Revise for History GCSE
The Modern World

Nigel Kelly   Alan Brooks-Tyreman

Heinemann

Heinemann Educational Publishers
Halley Court, Jordan Hill, Oxford OX2 8EJ
a division of Reed Educational & Professional Publishing Ltd

OXFORD MELBOURNE AUCKLAND
IBADAN JOHANNESBURG GABORONE
PORTSMOUTH NH (USA) CHICAGO BLANTYRE

Heinemann is a registered trademark of Reed Educational &
Professional Publishing Ltd

© Nigel Kelly and A G Brooks-Tryeman 1998
First published 1998

02 01 00 99 98
10 9 8 7 6 5 4 3 2 1

British Library Cataloguing in Publication Data is available from the British Library on request.

ISBN 0 435 10143 9

Typeset by Tech Set Ltd, Gateshead, Tyne & Wear
Printed and bound in Great Britain at The Bath Press, Bath
Cover Design by Threefold Design
Cover Photo by SuperStock

Acknowledgements

The publishers would like to thank the following for permission to reproduce photographs and illustrations.

p. 10 Punch Magazine; p. 16 Punch Magazine; p. 42 (top) The Times (bottom) Imperial War Museum; p. 51 David Low/London Evening Standard/Cartoons, University of Kent; p. 65 (top) David Low/London Evening Standard/Cartoons, University of Kent (bottom) Punch Magazine; p. 66 DavidLow/London Evening Standard/Cartoons, University of Kent; p. 74 AKG; p. 98 Corbis; p. 99 Corbis; p. 100 UPI/Corbis; p. 109 Peter Newark's American Pictures; p. 110 Peter Newark's American Pictures; p. 111 Washington Post; p. 112 Peter Newark's American Pictures; p. 143 (top) Magnum (bottom) Gerald Scarfe.

Contents

Introduction	4
The World, 1914–45	**7**
1 Why did Europe go to War in 1914?	7
2 First World War, 1914-18	12
3 Securing Peace, 1919-29	18
4 Road to War, 1929-39	27
5 Second World War, 1939-45	36
Germany, 1918–45	**44**
6 Weimar Republic, 1918-33	44
7 The Rise of Hitler	55
8 Nazis take Power	61
9 Hitler in Power	68
The USA, 1919–45	**78**
10 Isolation, 1919-24	78
11 The 'Boom' Years: the USA in the 1920s	85
12 The Wall Street Crash	95
13 The 'New Deal'	102
Russia and the Soviet Union, 1904–54	**114**
14 Russia in Crisis, 1904-17	114
15 The Bolsheviks Victory	122
16 Stalin in Power	128
The World, 1945–91	**135**
17 The Cold War	135

Introduction

What do I study in SHP History?
The Modern World History GCSE course is one of three History syllabuses studied at GCSE. (The others are Schools History Project and Social and Economic History.) Each exam board has a Modern World Study syllabus and there is great similarity between what is set.

Here is a summary of the examinations set by each board:

OCR (previously MEG)
Paper 1: 2 hours
Questions on the Core Content and the Depth Studies.

Core Content:
International Relations, 1919-89

Depth Studies:
Germany, 1918-45
Russia, 1905-41
The USA, 1919-41
China, 1945-90

There are three sections. In Section A you have to answer one of two questions on International Relations, 1919-89. In Sections B and C you have to answer questions on the Depth Studies. You will be expected to know about one of these Depth Studies and to answer three questions. Marks are given for your ability to recall, describe, analyse and explain.

Paper 2: 1 hour 30 minutes
This is a source-based investigation on a historical issue from the Core Content. Marks are focused on your ability to interpret representations and evaluate historical sources.

Coursework
You will do coursework on two Depth Studies (which must be different from the one you studied for Paper 1).

AQA/SEG
Paper 1: Coursework
You will do one of the following:
Social and Economic Developments in Britain, 1900-39
The First World War
The USA, 1918-41
The Second World War
Race relations in the USA and South Africa
Another approved topic

Paper 2: 1 hour 45 minutes
Questions on the three Study Units:
Peace to War, 1919-39
USA and USSR as World Superpowers, 1945-63
USA and USSR as World Superpowers, 1963-91

You will be expected to know about *two* of these units and to answer three questions. Each question has a source to study, but most marks are given for your ability to recall, describe, analyse and explain.

Paper 3: 1 hour 45 minutes
Questions on the Depth Studies:
Russia, 1917-41
Germany, 1918-39

You will be expected to know about both Depth Studies. You have to answer two questions. One question tests your ability to interpret representations and evaluate historical sources. The second question is concerned with recall, description, analysis and explanation.

AQA/ NEAB
Paper 1: 1 hour 45 minutes
Questions on Conflict in the Modern World.

A number of structured questions is set and the main focus is on recall, description, analysis and explanation.

Paper 2: 1 hour 45 minutes
Questions on Governments in Action.

1 Section A: Russia, 1900-56
   Germany, 1918-39
  Section B: USA, 1919-41
   Britain, 1905-51

You will be expected to answer two questions, one from Section A and one from Section B. So you need to know about one country in each section. The questions focus on testing your ability to interpret representations and evaluate historical sources.

Coursework
You will do one of the following:
International Co-operation
Modern Europe, Post-1945
The Arab/Israeli Dispute
Vietnam, Post-1939

NB This syllabus has an option of answering questions on one of the above topics in a Paper 3 (1 hour 15 minutes) instead of doing coursework.

Edexcel
Paper 1: 1 hour 45 minutes
Questions on the Outline Studies:
The Emergence of Modern Britain, 1868-1914
The Road to War, 1870-1914
Nationalism and Independence in India, 1900-49
The Impact of War in Britain, 1900-50
The Emergence of Modern China, 1911-70
The Soviet Union, 1928-91
The USA, 1941-80
Britain's Changing Role in the World, 1945-90
Superpower Relations, 1945-90
Conflict and the Quest for Peace in the Middle East, 1948-92

You will be expected to know about *two* of these Outline Studies and to answer two questions in total. Marks are given for your ability to recall, describe, analyse and explain.

Paper 2: 1 hour 30 minutes
Questions on Depth Studies:
The Russian Revolution, 1910-24
The War to End all Wars, 1914-18
The USA, 1929-41
Germany, 1930-9
The World at War, 1938-45
The End of Apartheid in South Africa, 1982-94
Conflict in Vietnam, 1963-75

You will be expected to answer two questions on separate Depth Studies. So you need to know about two of them. The questions focus on testing your ability to interpret representations and evaluate historical sources.

Coursework
You can do coursework on any programme of study related to the syllabus (but not on things you are going to answer questions on in the exam).

What sort of questions will I get?

The examination papers are designed to test four things:

1 Can you recall historical information to organise an answer using relevant facts?
2 Can you describe and explain events, changes and issues in history?
3 Can you explain similarities and differences between sources and comment on their usefulness and reliability?
4 Can you explain how different interpretations of the same event can exist?

All of the examination boards set two examination papers with a number of structured questions. (That means that they have parts to them. They are not just essays.) Often the questions have some sources to study before you answer the questions. What is on each paper varies from board to board, so make sure you know exactly what your exam is like.

What is in this revsion guide?

We have selected the topics which the vast majority of you study. So the revision guide covers:

The World, 1914-45 (including the two world wars and international relations).

Germany, 1918-45 (including the Weimar Republic and how the Nazis came to and stayed in power).

The USA, 1919-45 (including the years of 'boom and bust' and how economic problems were dealt with).

Russia and the Soviet Union, 1904-54 (including the overthrow of the Tsar and the USSR under Lenin and Stalin).

The World 1945-91 (including a study of international relations from the outbreak of the Cold War to the collapse of the Soviet Empire).

In each section you will find:

Topic summary

Sometimes studying history in depth can be confusing because you get to know so much detail that you lose sight of the 'big picture'. So we start each section with a summary of what the topic is about.

What do I need to know?

The revision guide then gives you a summary of what you need to know for the exam. Summary boxes are also included to give you a handy visual summary. When you have completed your revision you should be able to take a summary box and write at length about each point that is shown in it.

History of the topic

Here we give you the basic facts about the topic, but not in the same detail as in your textbook and notes. We are not telling you the whole story again, but instead are summarising it to make it easier for you to learn.

What do I know?

Once you have completed your revision you might like to test yourself to see how much you know. We have included a short self-assessment section so that you can see just how thorough your revision has been. Most of the questions can be answered from information given in the summary, but we also presume that you have been learning the information in your book and notes!

Using the sources

A vital part of any history course is being able to use sources. We have, therefore, included a number of 'using the sources' exercises in the book. Sometimes we give you even more help by adding hints on how to the answer the questions.

Exam type questions

You may be studying history because you love it and not care about how you do in the exam. For most students, however, what they really want is to do as well as possible in the examination. So we have given you lots of examples of the types of questions you will be asked together with some student answers.

Examiner's comments

The authors of this book are experienced SHP Senior Examiners and they have commented on each exam question answer. By reading their comments you will be able to see what is good and what is disappointing in the answer. Then you can make sure that any answer you give in the exam is much better.

What is the best way to revise?

1 Be organised
You can't revise properly if you don't have all the necessary material. So make sure that your work is in order and up to date.

2 Revise regularly
Revision is not something which you should leave until the last few weeks (or days!) before an exam. If you can learn as you go along then it will be much easier to take it all in before the final exam. Try to find a few minutes each week to go over what it is you have studied. If there is anything you haven't fully understood get it cleared up now!

3 Plan a proper revision timetable
The last few months of your course can be a stressful and worrying time. So make a sensible revision timetable and stick to it. Make sure you set yourself realistic targets. You know yourself better than anyone else and you know what it is you can do.

It's no good saying that you will do eight hour's revision on a certain day. You won't be able to do it and then you will get depressed. But you probably could manage four lots of one hour revision slots with a break to do something you enjoy in between each one. This is a much better way to revise anyway, because after an hour your concentration will start to go, so you need a break.

4 Use your guide
If you try to revise by simply reading your work you will soon get bored and you won't take it all in. So read a small section of your file, read our summary text and then make some simple revision notes. Read these through and when you think you know your work try extending the points in the summary boxes. Once you are happy with the topic, answer the 'What do I know?' section and then do the sources and examination question work. By then you should be well prepared.

5 Stay Cool
At examination time everyone is stressed. To do well you not only have to be well-prepared, but you also have to control your own feelings of panic. Stick to your revision timetable and practice answering questions. Then you'll be fine, but make sure you arrive for the examination in plenty of time. You have enough to do without worrying about being late.

6 Be lucky
Lucky people get questions in the examination on the very bits they have revised most thoroughly. Since we can't guarantee that this will happen to you, it's best to revise everything thoroughly. Then you are bound to be lucky!

Here's hoping the revision goes well, the exam goes even better and the results go best of all!

The World, 1914–45

1. Why did Europe go to War in 1914?

1

Topic Summary

The period 1900 to 1914 was was one in which rivalries between the Great Powers of Europe were so deep-rooted that there was no way of solving them except by means of a war. The main problem seemed to be the rise of Germany as a world power and the threat this posed to Britain and France. At the same time Russia and Austria-Hungary were on the brink of war.

2

What do I Need to Know?

You will need to know the reasons why the First World War happened. You will need to be able to sort these reasons into some kind of order of importance and to consider long-term and short-term causes as well as why war actually broke out in August 1914.

3

History of the Origins of the First World War

The rivalries

Economic rivalry

- Britain had been the first major industrial power. It had been called 'the Workshop of the World', but Britain's industrial growth was slowing down.
- German industry was fast becoming the most efficient and the highest producer of goods. Britain felt threatened by the growth of German industry.

Colonial rivalry

- Britain, France and Russia had huge empires. These were seen as a symbol of power and prestige, and a way of creating great wealth.
- After unification in 1870, Germany felt it had a right to a world-wide empire. Its leaders saw this as a way to prove that Germany was an important and strong world power.
- As most of the world was already controlled by Britain, France and Russia, or protected by the United States, the only way of creating a German empire was by going to war or threatening other powers.
- In 1905, Kaiser Wilhelm II visited Morocco, a French colony in Africa. The Kaiser claimed he supported Moroccan freedom. Really he wanted to take over from the French.
- In 1911, the Kaiser sent a gunboat to Agadir in Morocco. He was trying to break the alliance of Britain and France. In fact the crisis pushed the two countries closer together.

European territorial rivalry

- For many centuries, the Ottoman or Turkish Empire had controlled the south-west area of Europe called the Balkans. By 1900 the Turks were losing control of the area.
- Both Austria and Russia believed they had a right to replace the Turks in the Balkans. Both countries set about gaining allies in the region. It was an area of conflict.
- France wanted to recover the provinces of Alsace and Lorraine that was lost to Germany in the war of 1871.

Military problems

Alliance system

- Britain, France and Russia were increasingly concerned with the military power of Germany. These three decided to form an agreement called the Triple Entente.
- Germany and Austria-Hungary formed the Triple Alliance with Italy.
- When trouble did develop in the Balkans, the alliance system ensured that all the main nations of Europe were involved.

The arms race

- An arms race was developing between Britain and Germany. A new highly advanced battleship, the Dreadnought, meant all other warships were less effective.
- Between 1906 and 1914, Britain built 29 Dreadnoughts and Germany 17. In 1910 one British national newspaper ran a campaign demanding 'We want eight [Dreadnoughts] and we won't wait.'
- The arms race aroused passions and the desire for war.

Sarajevo and the assassination of Archduke Franz Ferdinand

- On 28 June Austria's Archduke Franz Ferdinand was visiting the Bosnian capital Sarajevo to inspect his troops. He was assassinated by Gavrilo Princip, a member of the Black Hand gang which wanted Serbia to be free of Austria-Hungary.
- Austria-Hungary blamed the Serbian government for the assassination. Austria demanded the Serbs give in to a series of tough demands.
- Serbia was protected by Russia, but Austria believed it could get what it wanted because of Germany's support.
- By September 1914 Britain, France and Russia were at war with Germany and Austria-Hungary. Of the six major European powers only Italy did not declare war. Eventually it sided with Britain, France and Russia. The Italians hoped to gain land if Austria-Hungary was defeated.

The Schlieffen Plan

- When France and Russia became allies, German military leaders knew they would have to fight the next war on two fronts. This had to be avoided at all costs.
- So, Count Schlieffen devised a plan. Germany would invade France and defeat it within six weeks (as had happened in 1871). Then it would deal with Russia, which would take six weeks to prepare its army.
- The plan had a major flaw. The German army had to go through Belgium to invade and defeat France. When this happened Britain joined the war to defend Belgium. Britain had signed an agreement in 1839 to defend Belgium if it was attacked. The Germans were surprised that Britain was prepared to go to war over a 'scrap of paper'.

Summary box

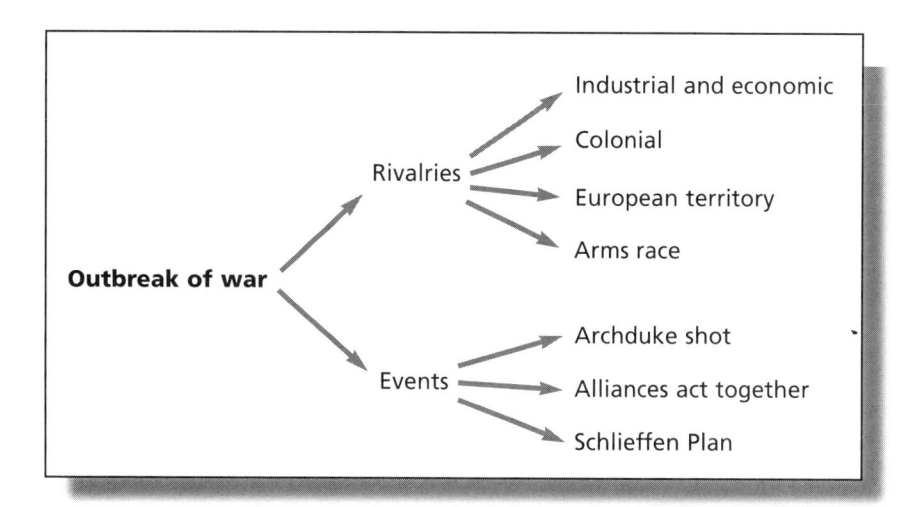

Outbreak of war
- Rivalries
  - Industrial and economic
  - Colonial
  - European territory
  - Arms race
- Events
  - Archduke shot
  - Alliances act together
  - Schlieffen Plan

Task Fill in the missing words in this spider diagram. Each letter is the beginning of the missing word.

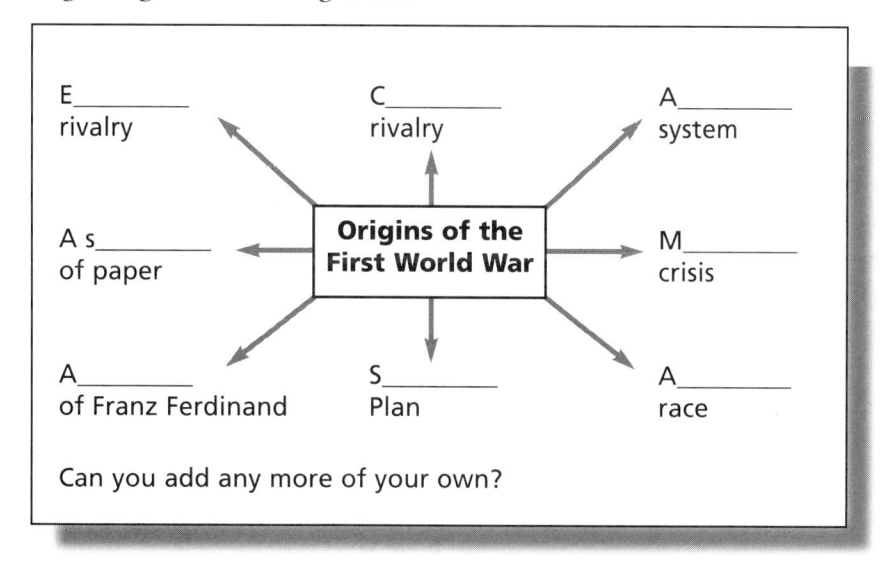

Origins of the First World War:
- E_____ rivalry
- C_____ rivalry
- A_____ system
- A s_____ of paper
- M_____ crisis
- A_____ of Franz Ferdinand
- S_____ Plan
- A_____ race

Can you add any more of your own?

Why did Europe go to War in 1914?

4. What do I Know?

Once you have revised this topic thoroughly you should be able to answer most of these questions without using your notes. How many can you get right?

1. What was the name of the alliance of Britain, France and Russia?
2. What was the name of the alliance of Germany, Italy and Austria-Hungary?
3. What is a Dreadnought?
4. Why were Dreadnoughts so important?
5. Which area of France had Germany taken control of after the 1871 war?
6. Which country had the biggest empire in 1900?
7. What happened at Agadir in 1911?
8. Who was Kaiser of Germany in 1900?
9. The German Kaiser said his country wanted its 'place in the sun'. What do you think he meant?
10. Who devised the German war plan?
11. Which country had Britain promised to protect since 1839?
12. Where is Sarajevo?
13. Who shot the Archduke Franz Ferdinand?
14. Which throne was Franz Ferdinand heir to?
15. Which country did Austria-Hungary blame for the Archduke's murder?

My score ....

What was important about:
- The alliance system
- The assassination of the Archduke Franz Ferdinand
- The 1839 agreement between Britain and Belgium?

5. Exam Type Question

Here is the sort of cartoon that might appear in your exam paper. Study it carefully and then answer the question that follows.

◀ British cartoon showing Belgium being bullied by the German Kaiser.

10

Why did Europe go to War in 1914?

> How useful is the cartoon to an historian studying the topic of the causes of the First World War? Explain your answer fully.

Answer

I think the cartoon is very useful because it gives us information as to why the British government went to war. This was because Germany attacked Belgium, which went against the 1839 agreement. The source also shows us the aggressive nature of Germany, the large stick showing German power. We would need to be careful as obviously this source is by a British cartoonist and may be part of a propaganda campaign against the Germans. We can see this because the German is being portrayed as a big bully and the boy (representing Belgium) looks sweet and innocent, but determined. However, the source does not tell us about many other causes of the war, such as colonial rivalry, economic rivalry or the assassination of the Archduke Franz Ferdinand in Sarajevo. It is a good source but an historian would need more.

Examiner's Comments

I am certain that this student knows a great about the causes of the First World War. The clear points made in the answer show an understanding of the cartoon and what is missing. It uses the imagery from the cartoon to explain the points, which is very important to score high marks. The only slight reservation I have is the lack of specific detail on the other causes of war. However the overall answer shows understanding of bias and would be given 5 or 6 marks. Full marks would have been given if the candidate had said that the source was useful as an example of British propaganda.

Practice Question

Now try to answer the question yourself. Remember that to answer a question on usefulness you need to look at the following points:

1. What information do(es) the source(s) contain? Is it relevant to the question set?
2. What information is missing from the source(s)? Is this missing information vital, or can the historian get most of what they need from the source(s) provided?
3. You might need to assess the reliability of the source. However do not make the mistake of suggesting a source is of no use because it is unreliable. For example, in the question above the answer should have said that this source was useful to show us how propaganda was used to make the British anti-German.

2. First World War, 1914–18

1. Topic Summary

The First World War was the first 'Total War'. That is, it was the first war to include civilians as well as the military in the day-to-day events. Although most people expected a quick war, it was to last for four years and result in the deaths of millions of young men. Much of the fighting in the war took place on the French and Belgium border in an area known as the Western Front. This is where most exam boards concentrate their answers.

2. What do I Need to Know?

You will be expected to know why the war did not finish before Christmas 1914 and how the system of trenches developed. You will need to know the nature of trench warfare, both in terms of military strategy and its effects on the soldiers involved. You will also need to assess the role of new weapons in the fighting.

In terms of the effects on civilians in Britain, you need to explain how this war was different from any previous conflict, especially the effect on the role of women in society. You need to be aware of the measures taken by the government to protect the civilians, and how effective they were.

3. History of the First World War

Why was the war not over by Christmas?

The Schlieffen Plan failed. It failed for several reasons.
- The Belgians held up the Germans rather than letting them go straight through Belgium to France.
- The British Expeditionary Force was able to reach Belgium and help delay the Germans.
- The Russians were able to mobilise their troops in just 10 days, not the six weeks as expected.
- As the Germans retreated to areas that were easier to defend, they set up a series of trenches that stretched from the English Channel to the Swiss border. The British and French in turn set up trenches to protect their men. The great advance had been halted.

On hearing news of the failure, Von Moltke, commander of the German army, told the Kaiser 'Sire, we have lost the war', but the war went on for four more years.

Summary box 1

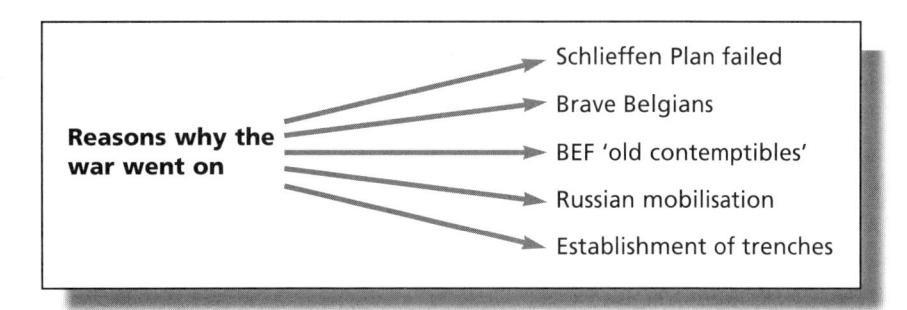

Reasons why the war went on:
- Schlieffen Plan failed
- Brave Belgians
- BEF 'old contemptibles'
- Russian mobilisation
- Establishment of trenches

Trench warfare

Much of the fighting on the Western Front involved trying to capture enemy trenches. Various methods were used.
- Before an attack, the enemy trench would be bombarded by shells to weaken the enemy's resolve.
- The soldiers would then climb out of their trenches (going 'over the top') and advance towards the enemy across 'No Man's Land'.
- The attackers would have to overcome many obstacles, such as barbed wire, shell holes, mud and water, and even dead bodies.
- As they advanced across 'No Man's Land', they were often easy targets for the enemy's deadly machine-gun fire. Even when an enemy trench was captured usually there were not enough men to hold it.

The position of the troops in the trenches moved little in four years and neither side appeared to be able to win the war by direct attack. To end this stalemate each side tried to wear the enemy down. This was called 'attrition'.

Summary box 2

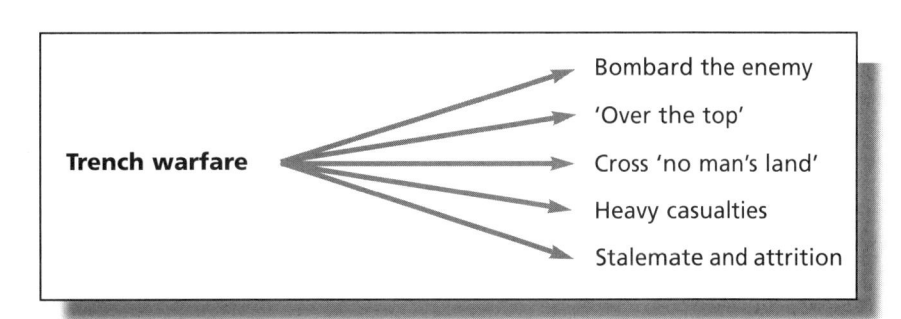

Trench warfare:
- Bombard the enemy
- 'Over the top'
- Cross 'no man's land'
- Heavy casualties
- Stalemate and attrition

New weapons

New weapons were needed to break the deadlock.
- In April 1915 the Germans first used gas as a weapon. However gas-masks were soon developed to protect soldiers against the gas. Also there was always the danger of the wind changing direction and the gas blowing back on your own men.
- Tanks came into use in 1916. Sometimes they were very successful. But they were slow, clumsy, easily got stuck in the mud, and they overheated.

First World War, 1914–18

- Airplanes were used to spy on enemy positions. But the technology had not yet been developed for planes to attack and bomb enemy positions.
- The new weapons had a minimal effect on the main strategies of the generals, who still believed in bombarding the enemy with artillery and then attacking with infantry soldiers.

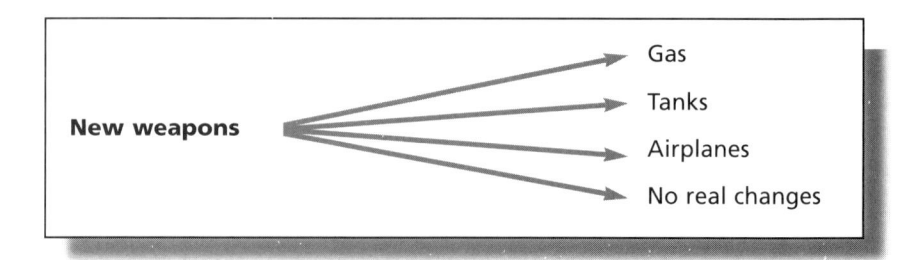

Summary box 3

New weapons:
- Gas
- Tanks
- Airplanes
- No real changes

Physical and psychological effects

- For many men fighting in the trenches was a terrifying experience. The horrors of warfare caused some of them to suffer irreversible psychological problems.
- Soldiers spent about 10 to 14 days at a time in the front line and they could not rest or sleep properly due to the regular shelling.
- Plagues of rats, lice and fleas caused disease and some soldiers got trench foot, from the waterlogged trenches. Bronchitis and chest complaints were also common.

Summary box 4

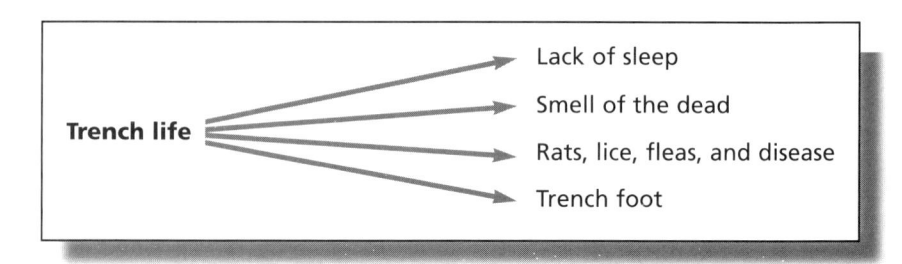

Trench life:
- Lack of sleep
- Smell of the dead
- Rats, lice, fleas, and disease
- Trench foot

The war at home

- In the first few months of the war, over a million men volunteered to join the British army. They were persuaded by the appeal that 'Your country needs you'.
- Men joined up out of patriotism, fear of being called cowards, the promise of adventure, or the need for a job. Propaganda was used constantly.
- Conscription was introduced in December 1915 when it was clear that the war would go on and that the volunteers would not be enough. People at home were now also realising that the war was not the glorious adventure they had first thought it would be.
- Women were needed and encouraged to take over the jobs of the men who went to war. Their role in factories, as nurses and in food production became essential for victory.

- Those at home suffered from German air-raids, mainly on the eastern coast. At first they were shelled from ships, bombed from the air by Zeppelins and later by planes, though casualties were light compared to the Second World War.
- German submarines blockaded Britain's ports and attacked merchant ships carrying food. This policy of 'unrestricted warfare' brought the British close to starvation and surrender (in 1917 rationing was introduced. Britain had been just six weeks away from defeat.) But it also helped bring the US into the war.
- Britain was saved by the convoy system, depth charges, mines and the use of Q-ships.
- The government took greater control of everyday life. The Defence of the Realm Act (DORA) was used to censor newspapers, water down beer, control hours and places of work etc.

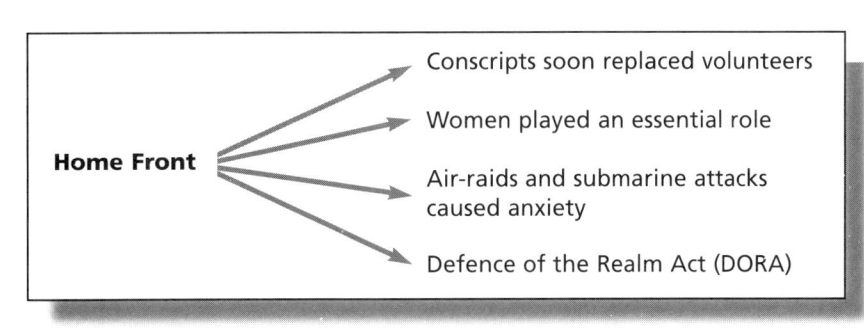

Summary box 5

Home Front
- Conscripts soon replaced volunteers
- Women played an essential role
- Air-raids and submarine attacks caused anxiety
- Defence of the Realm Act (DORA)

What do I Know?

Once you have revised this topic thoroughly you should be able to answer most of these questions without using your notes. How many can you get right?

1. Which German plan failed, creating the need for the trenches?
2. Give one reason for the failure of the plan.
3. When did people expect the war to finish?
4. Who was the commander of the German army in 1914?
5. What was the 'contemptible little army'?
6. What was the area between the two sets of trenches called?
7. What was the name given to the rotting of feet caused by water in the trenches?
8. Who was in charge of recruitment into the British army?
9. Which new weapon sometimes affected your own troops as well as the enemy's?
10. When was conscription introduced in Britain?
11. What were Zeppelins?
12. How did Britain counter the threat from German submarines?
13. What does DORA stand for?
14. When was rationing introduced?
15. When did the war end?

My score ....

What was important about:
- The Schlieffen Plan
- Stalemate on the Western Front
- DORA
- Conscription?

First World War, 1914–18

5. Key Dates to Learn

1914	First World War begins
1915	First use of gas and tanks
1915	Conscription introduced
1916	The Battle of the Somme
1917	Russia leaves war; America joins Allies
1918	First World War ends, Allies are victorious.

6. Exam Type Question

Here is the sort of question you might be asked in an exam paper. Look closely at the answer given and the examiner's comments on it. Then answer the question yourself.

> Look at the cartoon below. How reliable is this cartoon to an historian studying the topic of the attitude of the soldiers during the First World War? Explain your answer fully. **(6 marks)**

Major-General (addressing the men before practising an attack behind the lines). "I WANT YOU TO UNDERSTAND THAT THERE IS A DIFFERENCE BETWEEN A REHEARSAL AND THE REAL THING. THERE ARE THREE ESSENTIAL DIFFERENCES: FIRST, THE ABSENCE OF THE ENEMY. NOW *(turning to the Regimental Sergeant-Major)* WHAT IS THE SECOND DIFFERENCE?"

Sergeant-Major. "THE ABSENCE OF THE GENERAL, SIR."

▲ A British cartoon showing the attitude of soldiers to their military leaders.

Answer

I do not think that the cartoon is a very reliable source because it is a cartoon and cartoons are made to be humorous. However the cartoon must have an element of truth to make the joke funny. The source was published in 1917. This is during the war. This means we have to be careful as the British government had censorship powers over newspapers. The government must have had a reason to allow a cartoon that attacks the generals to be published.

It may have been allowed to suggest that the government was also frustrated by the lack of success in the war and the high numbers of casualities. This may question it's reliability. However the cartoon does reflect the views of many of the soldiers who were doing the real fighting whilst the generals were merely 'playing' at being at war. It is also, of course, reliable as an example of the sort of feelings that some people had towards the war in 1917.

Examiner's Comments

This answer shows a good grasp of reliability. It shows that the student understands the different factors affecting a source's reliability. It tries to understand the motivation behind the source. This is essential. However, it could do with a little more direct reference to what is in the cartoon. This answer would be given 5 marks.

Practice Question

Now answer the question yourself. Remember that to answer a question on reliability you need to look at the following points:

1. Who wrote/made the source? Do they have a reason to be biased?
2. When was the source written or made? Are there any special circumstances that might affect the reliability of the source?
3. Why was the source made or written? Did the author/artist have a specific reason for saying what they say?
4. Reliability is all about trust. Do any of the words or images suggest that you cannot trust the source?
5. Remember that if you suggest a source is reliable/unreliable try to explain what it is in the source that shows this.

3. Securing Peace, 1919–29

1. Topic Summary

When the war ended in 1918 decisions had to be made about how the defeated nations (Germany, Austria-Hungary, Bulgaria and Turkey) were to be treated. Those decisions were made in a series of conferences held in Versailles in France shortly after the war. The treaties which were drawn up as a result were designed to keep peace in Europe for the foreseeable future. Over the next ten years further steps were taken to try to promote international agreement and remove possible causes of disagreement.

2. What do I Need to Know?

The most commonly asked question in this section is why Germany was treated so harshly after the war and whether the desire for revenge was a major cause of the Second World War. You will need to know details of the personalities involved and their feelings and comment on whether the treaties were fair. You will also have to know about the League of Nations and international agreements in this period to show that there were genuine attempts to keep peace.

3. History of the Attempts to Establish Peace

Redrawing the map: the Versailles settlement

People and issues

- Although 32 countries were represented at the peace talks the decisions were really made by the 'Big Three' – Britain, France and the USA – though sometimes historians talk of the 'Big Four', which includes Italy.
- President Wilson hoped his Fourteen Points would be the basis of peace, including arms reduction, the setting up of a League of Nations and allowing people to govern themselves (self-determination).
- Wilson hoped that he could help draw up treaties which would keep the peace and prevent his country from having to send soldiers to fight in Europe in the future.
- Georges Clemenceau of France, however, wanted revenge for French losses in the war and Germany made so weak that it would never be a threat to France again.
- David Lloyd George of Britain wanted Germany punished, but he was also worried that too harsh a treaty would lead to Germany fighting a war of revenge in future years.
- Vittorio Orlando of Italy wanted to gain territory which Italy and Austria-Hungary disputed. He thought that as Italy had fought on the winning side it would be given this land.

Summary box 1

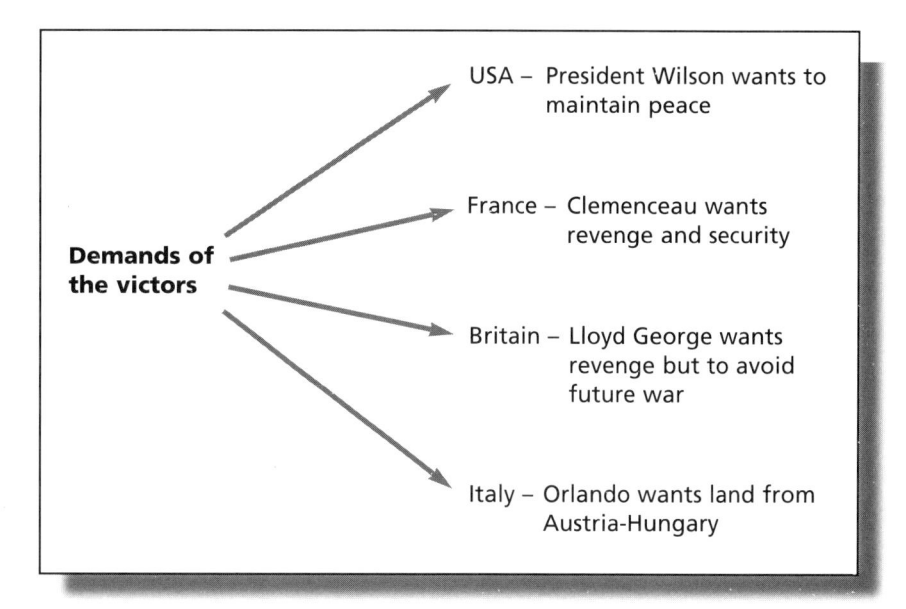

Demands of the victors:
- USA – President Wilson wants to maintain peace
- France – Clemenceau wants revenge and security
- Britain – Lloyd George wants revenge but to avoid future war
- Italy – Orlando wants land from Austria-Hungary

The settlements

The Treaty of Versailles

Clemenceau was happiest with the Treaty of Versailles because Germany was dealt with very firmly.

German military power was weakened:

- The German army was to be no larger than 100,000 men, the size of its navy limited and its air force disbanded. It was not allowed to have any tanks, submarines or heavy artillery.
- To protect the French border a demilitarized zone 50 kilometres (30 miles) wide was established on the east bank of the Rhine.

German territory was reduced:

- All Germany's colonies were taken and given to the victorious powers as mandates.
- German land was given to Belgium, France, Denmark and Poland, with the League of Nations looking after several ex-German cities. In all, Germany gave up about 13 per cent of its land size. Most importantly, by giving West Prussia to Poland the peace-makers divided Germany into two.

Germany was forced to pay for the war:

- The Allies made Germany agree to Article 231 (the 'War Guilt' Clause) which said that the war was Germany's fault. This gave the legal excuse for making the Germans pay reparations. This was set at £6,600 million, to be paid in instalments over 42 years.

- These payments were demanded even though the German economy was in ruins after the war and the treaty took away German merchant ships and railway engines. Much of the land lost by Germany contained valuable coal and iron deposits (which were now no longer available to the Germans).

German pride was destroyed:

- The Germans had fought the war to show their military strength. Now they were forced to agree that the war had all been their fault and they should pay for it.
- Germany also suffered a blow to its pride because of the restrictions placed on it.
- Germany was not allowed to negotiate the terms of the treaty, but instead had to accept a 'Diktat'. When they said that they would not sign the treaty, the Germans were told that if they did not the Allies would occupy Germany.

Summary box 2

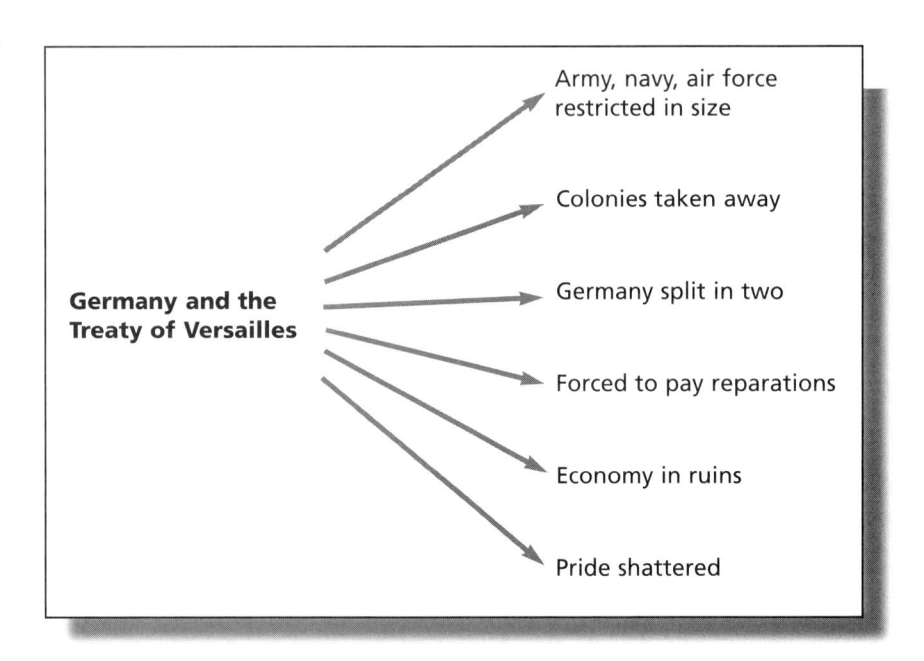

Germany and the Treaty of Versailles:
- Army, navy, air force restricted in size
- Colonies taken away
- Germany split in two
- Forced to pay reparations
- Economy in ruins
- Pride shattered

Was the treatment of Germany fair?

Whether the treaty was fair is a question historians have to decide for themselves. You need to make up your own mind, but just think about these points.

- What would the Germans have done if they had won the war? (In 1871 they had made the French pay large sums in reparations when they beat them in the Franco-Prussian War.)
- Could the Allies have just forgotten about what happened in the war and carried on as if nothing had happened? What would the people of France and Britain, whose men had been killed, have thought of this?

Treatment of the other defeated nations

Austria-Hungary (I)
Before the war Austria-Hungary had been a vast multi-racial empire of 51 million people. This empire was split into two separate countries and in the **Treaty of St Germain** in 1919 (with Austria) the Allies tried to follow the policy of self-determination by using land from Austria-Hungary to set up two new countries, Czechoslovakia and Yugoslavia, and to reform the old Poland. Land was also given to Italy and Romania. Austria was reduced to just 6 million people and limitations were placed on the size of its military forces.

Austria-Hungary (II)
In the **Treaty of Trianon** in 1920 (with Hungary) Hungarian land was given to Yugoslavia, Czechoslovakia and Romania. Restrictions were placed on the size of the Hungarian military forces.

Defeat in the First World War

Bulgaria
By the **Treaty of Neuilly** in 1919 Bulgaria gave land to Yugoslavia, Greece and Romania. The Bulgarian army was limited to 20,000 men and Bulgaria had to pay reparations.

Turkey
The Turks were dealt with very severely in the **Treaty of Sevres** in 1920. Land was given to Greece, Italy and France and the new League of Nations took control of the Turkish capital, Constantinople, and surrounding areas. All Turkish colonies were taken away, Turkey was disarmed and made to pay reparations.

The Turks were so angry that they refused to accept the terms and rose in rebellion under Mustapha Kemal. New terms were agreed in the **Treaty of Lausanne** in 1923. Constantinople and some of its old colonies were returned to Turkey, reparations and disarmament were dropped. At the same time Mustapha Kemal overthrew the Sultan and made himself President. The old Turkish (Ottoman) Empire was over.

Keeping the peace

The League of Nations

- In January 1918 President Wilson had called for 'a general association of nations' to prevent further wars. This organisation was set up in the Treaty of Versailles.
- It tried to keep peace by having 'Collective Security', i.e. all nations working together to provide peace and safety for everyone. This was to be done by:
    - Reducing the number of weapons in the world
    - Settling disputes by peaceful means instead of fighting
    - Encouraging co-operation between nations.

- These aims were set out in the first part of the treaty, which is usually called the Covenant (rules) of the League. The League would settle disputes by:
  - Arbitration by a neutral country
  - Taking the matter to the International Court of Justice
  - The Council carrying out an inquiry.

Summary box 3

The organisations of the League of Nations
- Secretariat – to carry out the administration
- Assembly – all nations to discuss international issues
- Council – committee to discuss international issues
- Court of International Justice – to settle international disputes
- International Labour Organisation – to help improve working conditions around the world
- Special Commissions – teams of experts from around the world to deal with specific problems such as refugees

Weaknesses of the League

Although the League was set up to maintain peace and improve co-operation between countries, there were several reasons why it found this difficult.

- Membership. The League had some important countries missing from its membership. The USA never joined, the Soviet Union and Germany were excluded at first, and other nations left when they disagreed with the League's policies.
- The League had no army. Only if other sanctions failed would the countries join together to take military action. In practice the League never took military action.
- Major powers acted on their own. During the 1930s it became clear that some of the major powers would rather take their own actions than work through the League.

The Work of the League in the 1920s

During the 1920s the League had some important successes.

- In 1920 it settled a dispute between Sweden and Finland over the Aaland Islands.
- In 1920 it helped divide Upper Silesia between Poland and Germany.
- In 1922 it helped provide financial aid for Austria.

- In 1925 it stopped Greece invading Bulgaria.
- The commissions met regularly and carried out important work, particularly in the settlement of refugees and the trade in illegal drugs.

But there were several warnings that the League would have problems if faced with opposition.

- In 1920 the Poles seized Vilna, the capital of Lithuania, and the League was not able to force the Poles to return it.
- In 1923 Lithuania seized Memel, a town under international control. Again the League could not force its return.
- In 1923 Italy bombarded Corfu in a dispute with Greece. The League opposed Italy but the Council of Ambassadors (a committee of wartime Allies set up to make sure countries stood by the 1919 treaties) made the Greeks pay compensation.

So the first time the League had come into conflict with a major power it had failed.

Making treaties

In the years following the Versailles Conference, there were a number of treaties between the major powers. Each one tried to remove a threat to world peace

- The Washington Conference 1921. The USA, Britain, France, Japan and Italy agreed to limit the number of their battleships. This was to stop another arms race like that before the First World War.
- The Geneva Protocol 1923. The League tried to stop future wars by asking countries to agree that any country which refused arbitration would be labelled an aggressor and every nation in the League would act against it. However, Britain did not agree because it feared its empire could be drawn into war.
- The Dawes Plan 1924. To help Germany recover and to stop poor relations between Germany and France new terms were set up for the payment of reparations. A further agreement, the Young Plan, was signed in 1929.
- The Locarno Treaties 1925. Britain, France, Germany, Belgium and Italy agreed to guarantee the national boundaries as set out in the Treaty of Versailles. This was to remove the threat of future wars to regain lost territory.
  Treaties between Germany, Poland and Czechoslovakia in which Germany promised not to use force were also confirmed. In 1926 Germany joined the League.
- The Kellogg-Briand Pact 1928. Sixty-five nations signed an agreement not to go to war except in self-defence. This was aimed at preventing war, but showed the weakness of the League, because that is what it was supposed to do anyway!
- Young Plan 1929. This plan continued the practice of removing potential threats to peace and helping to promote prosperity. Germany was having difficulties paying its reparations, despite

the help it was receiving as a result of the Dawes Plan. Between 1924 and 1929 Germany had received over 25 billion marks in loans from abroad, but had paid 22 billion marks in reparations. The Young Plan extended the time Germany had to pay the loans to 59 years, at an average of 2 billion marks a year. Germany could also postpone payments in times of economic hardship.

Summary box 4

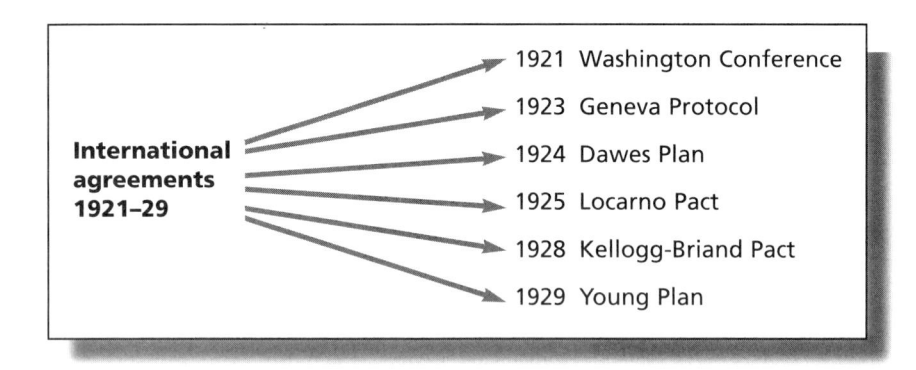

International agreements 1921–29
- 1921 Washington Conference
- 1923 Geneva Protocol
- 1924 Dawes Plan
- 1925 Locarno Pact
- 1928 Kellogg-Briand Pact
- 1929 Young Plan

4 What do I know?

Once you have revised this topic thoroughly you should be able to answer most of these questions without using your notes. How many can you get right

1. Who were the 'Big Three'?
2. What was self-determination?
3. After Versailles what was the maximum size of the German army?
4. How much did Germany have to pay in reparations?
5. Which treaty reduced Austria to six million people?
6. When was the Treaty of St Trianon?
7. Which treaty replaced the Treaty of Sevres?
8. Who was Turkey's first President?
9. What does 'Collective Security' mean?
10. Which body in the League of Nations was a court to settle disputes?
11. Which major power never joined the League of Nations?
12. Which country received economic aid from the League in 1922?
13. Why did Britain oppose the Geneva Protocol?
14. What was the purpose of the Dawes Plan?
15. What did Kellogg and Briand try to achieve?

My score ………

What was important about:
- The War Guilt Clause
- West Prussia
- Arbitration
- The Locarno Treaties?

Securing Peace, 1919–29

5 Exam Type Question

Study the source below. What can we learn about the Treaty of Versailles from this source? **(10 marks)**

▲ A cartoon about the Treaty of Versailles printed in the British newspaper, the *Daily Express*, in May 1919.

Answer 1

I don't think we can learn very much from this source because it is just a cartoon, and it is British – so it's biased because the British did not like the Germans.

Answer 2

We can learn a great deal from this source. First of all, the fact that Germany is being held tight by a fist of the Allied countries means that it had to be forced to accept the terms of the treaty. Then there is the fact that the Big Four are administering the medicine, which fits in with what I know about Lloyd-George, Clemenceau, Wilson and, to some extent, Orlando drawing up the treaty.

The most useful thing, however, is that the treaty is presented as a pill being forced down Germany's throat. I know that the Germans would not accept the treaty and called it a Diktat. But in this cartoon the treaty is shown as medicine. Obviously medicine is supposed to be good for you, so someone at the time thought that the treaty was a good thing, even though the Germans didn't think so. This might be just the *Daily Express*'s opinion, or it might show the feelings in Britain at large.

Securing Peace, 1919–29

Examiner's Comments: Answer 1

This is a very weak answer. It falls into the trap of rejecting the source because it is a cartoon. It also makes accusations of bias without any proof from the source or example of how this bias affects what is in the cartoon. I would give 1–2 marks at best.

Answer 2

This is a cracking answer! The candidate looks at the detail in the source, explores what it shows and uses impressive knowledge to support the answer. Then the answer looks at the overall meaning of the cartoon. The suggestion that from this cartoon we can learn that some people thought that the treaty was good for Germany is very impressive. I think this is worth full marks.

Practice Question

Have a look at the cartoon, re-read Answer 2 and then see how well you can do it – without copying Answer 2!

4. Road to War, 1929–39

1. Topic Summary

By 1929 the world seemed far from war. The League of Nations was working to keep peace and countries were signing treaties to try to improve relations and remove potential causes of war. But the reality was different. The League of Nations had already shown signs of weakness when dealing with major powers and there were to be even greater challenges ahead. First Japan and then Italy showed how ineffective the League was. Finally, the great resentment in Germany at the way the country had been treated at Versailles and the growing ambitions of Hitler helped bring war – despite the attempts of the British Prime Minister, Neville Chamberlain, to prevent it.

2. What do I Need to Know?

The most important thing in this section is to be able to explain why the relatively peaceful situation in 1929 deteriorated into war in 1939. This can be explained by the economic crisis that occurred in 1929, the failure of the League of Nations, the unresolved problems caused by the Treaty of Versailles, German resentment and ambitions, and the failure of the policy of appeasement followed by Britain and France in the late 1930s.

The economic crisis

In 1929 the United States went into recession after the Wall Street Crash. The fact that the USA was the wealthiest country in the world but could not afford to trade abroad was to have a major impact on other nations. One of these was Japan, which looked to solve its economic problems by military conquest.

Japan and Manchuria

In 1931 the Japanese decided to take over the Japanese province of Manchuria. They did this for a number of reasons:

- Japanese industry had been hard hit by the loss of American markets and it needed to find new markets.
- Manchuria had important raw materials, such as coal and iron ore.
- Japan was short of living space for its population.
- Japan claimed that the Manchurian railway (which they protected) was being attacked by the Chinese.

Manchuria belonged to China and the Chinese appealed to the League. This was a serious test for the League. How did it react?

- Early in 1932 it set up a Commission under Lord Lytton. The Commission condemned what the Japanese had done.

- Japan carried on capturing parts of Manchuria (which it had renamed Manchukuo) and left the League.
- The League took no further action.
- In 1937 Japan launched attacks on other parts of China.

Consequences of the attack:

- Japan captured Manchuria and had a base for future attacks on China.
- The League had been shown to be weak and not prepared to take action when the interests of its major members (Britain and France) were not at stake.

Summary box 1

The Japanese invasion of Manchuria

Why?	What happened?	Consequences
Space for population	Manchurian railway attacked	Manchuria becomes Japanese possession
Raw materials	Japanese invasion	League looks weak
New markets	Lytton Commission	
	Japan leaves League	

Italy and Abyssinia

The failure of the League to take decisive action against Japan in 1932 did not go unnoticed in Italy, and in 1935 the Italian leader, Mussolini, decided to invade Abyssinia in Africa. He did this because:

- Italy already had possessions in Africa around Abyssinia.
- Mussolini wanted revenge for Abyssinia defeating Italy in the Battle of Adowa in 1898.
- Mussolini wanted to build a great Italian empire like the old Roman Empire.
- Abyssinian tribesmen had killed 30 Italians in a border skirmish in 1934.

The Italians invaded in October 1935 using modern weapons, such as aircraft and poison gas. The Abyssinians were soon in retreat and their leader, Haile Selassie, went to the League of Nations to ask for help. How did the League react?

- The League decided that the Italians were the aggressors.
- Economic sanctions were applied.

But:

- Coal, oil and steel were excluded from the sanctions.
- Not all countries applied sanctions.

- Britain and France did not stop Mussolini using the Suez Canal to reach Abyssinia
- In December 1935 Britain and France proposed that Mussolini should get two-thirds of Abyssinia if he stopped fighting (the Hoare-Laval Pact). This plan was devised to keep Mussolini 'sweet' because Britain and France wanted his support against the growing threat of Hitler. But there was such opposition to it that it was dropped.

Once it became clear that Britain and France were actually working against official League policy, the other nations in the League withdrew their sanctions. Mussolini completed the conquest of Abyssinia in 1936 and Emperor Haile Selassie went into exile.

Consequences of the attack:

- Abyssinia became an Italian possession.
- The League was totally discredited. Not only had it failed to act effectively, but its most powerful members had acted against it.
- Mussolini did not side with Britain and France but instead signed the Rome-Berlin Axis with Germany in 1936, and in the next year left the League.
- With the League discredited Britain and France now had to look for other ways to keep peace.

Summary box 2

The Italian invasion of Abyssinia

Why?	What happened?	Consequences
Building an empire	Italian invasion with modern weapons	Abyssinia becomes an Italian possession
Revenge for Adowa	Haile Selassie appeals to League	League destroyed as an effective peace-keeping force
Attacks on Italians	League imposes sanctions	Mussolini leaves League
	Hoare-Laval Pact	Britain and France look to other ways to keep peace

The threat of Germany, 1933–9

During the 1930s Germany became more and more of a threat to world peace. Why was this?

- The Germans resented their losses at Versailles. They hated being blamed for the war, having to pay for it and for losing land which split the country in two.

- In 1929 Germany, like many other countries, went into economic recession. During the prosperous late 1920s the German people had been more prepared to accept the Treaty of Versailles. They were less prepared to do so now.
- In 1933 Hitler came to power in Germany. He hated the Treaty of Versailles and promised that he would regain Germany's lost land and restore its military might. It was Hitler's aggressive foreign policy which helped bring about the outbreak of the Second World War.

Steps to war : 1931–6

- In 1931 sixty-one nations met at a conference to discuss disarmament. The conference ended in failure. Germany had already walked out of the conference before it finished. In 1933 Germany also left the League of Nations. From 1933 Hitler began building a new air force (the Luftwaffe) and introduced conscription. Then he began re-equipping the army and navy.
- In 1934 Hitler began making plans to occupy Austria. He was stopped by Mussolini, who was not yet Hitler's ally. In 1935 Mussolini signed the Stresa Front with Britain and France to guarantee the terms of the Treaty of Versailles.
- In 1935 Germany retook possession of the Saar coalfields which had been under control of the League since 1919.
- In 1936 Hitler installed military forces inside the demilitarized zone along the Rhine. This was forbidden by the Treaty of Versailles. But Britain and France took no action. They thought that Hitler was only 'marching into his own back yard'.
- In the same year Mussolini and Hitler signed the Rome-Berlin Axis and German forces fought in the Spanish Civil War, where the Luftwaffe in particular gained valuable experience in war.

Why didn't Britain and France stop Hitler increasing German power? There were several reasons why no action was taken.

- Many people in Britain thought that Germany had been harshly treated at Versailles and that it had a right to restore its military power.
- Hitler was anti-communist, which for some British politicians was a reason to support him, because they saw communist Russia as a bigger threat than Nazi Germany.
- Standing up to Hitler might lead to war and people remembered the horrors of the First World War.
- Britain and France were both suffering from economic recession. Neither of them could afford a war and both needed to carry out extensive modernisation of their armed forces before they could fight a war.

Summary box 3

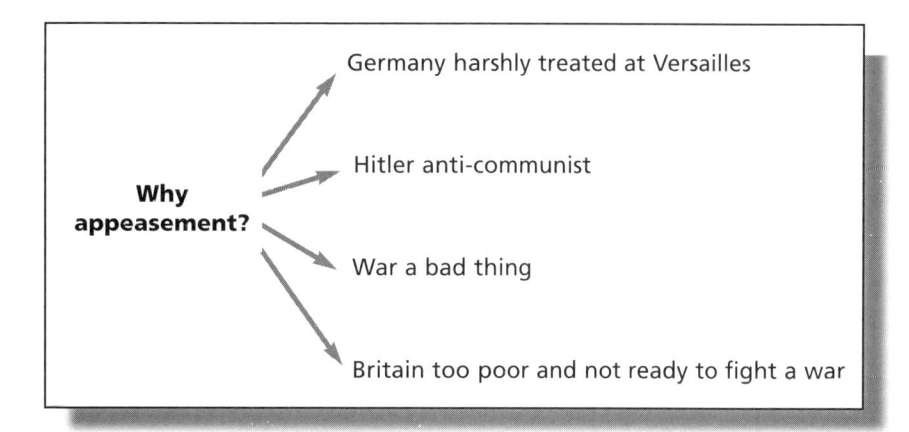

Why appeasement?
- Germany harshly treated at Versailles
- Hitler anti-communist
- War a bad thing
- Britain too poor and not ready to fight a war

It was for these reasons that Britain in particular followed a policy of appeasement in the late 1930s. This was the policy adopted by the Prime Minister, Neville Chamberlain, who preferred to pacify Hitler by negotiation rather than go to war.

Steps to war: 1937–9

- In 1937 Hitler extended the Rome-Berlin Axis by bringing Japan into the alliance in the Anti-Comintern Pact.
- In 1938 he occupied Austria and joined it to Germany (this 'Anschluss' was expressly forbidden by the Treaty of Versailles). Britain and France accepted a plebiscite as proof of Austrian agreement
- In 1938 Hitler began making threats to invade Czechoslovakia unless it handed over the German-speaking Sudetenland. Neville Chamberlain had two meetings with Hitler but could not reach agreement.
- Then in September 1938, Germany, Italy, France and Britain met at Munich and reached agreement that Hitler should have the Sudentenland (neither Czechoslovakia nor the Soviet Union were invited). In return Hitler said that he had no more 'territorial demands'.
- When Chamberlain returned to Britain he received a hero's welcome. He had saved the country from war and said that he had achieved 'peace in our time'.
- Then in March 1939 Hitler broke his promise and occupied the rest of Czechoslovakia. Chamberlain knew that war was near and speeded up British re-armament.
- Poland seemed next on Hitler's 'hit list' and both Britain and France guaranteed to help Poland if Hitler threatened.
- In August 1939 Hitler and Stalin signed a Nazi-Soviet Pact agreeing not to attack each other. Stalin knew it would give him time to build up his forces before the inevitable German invasion (and give him half of Poland). Hitler knew that he could now occupy western Poland without fear of attack by Russia.
- On 1 September 1939 Germany invaded Poland. Britain and France declared war two days later, but there was little they could do to save Poland.

Road to War, 1929–39

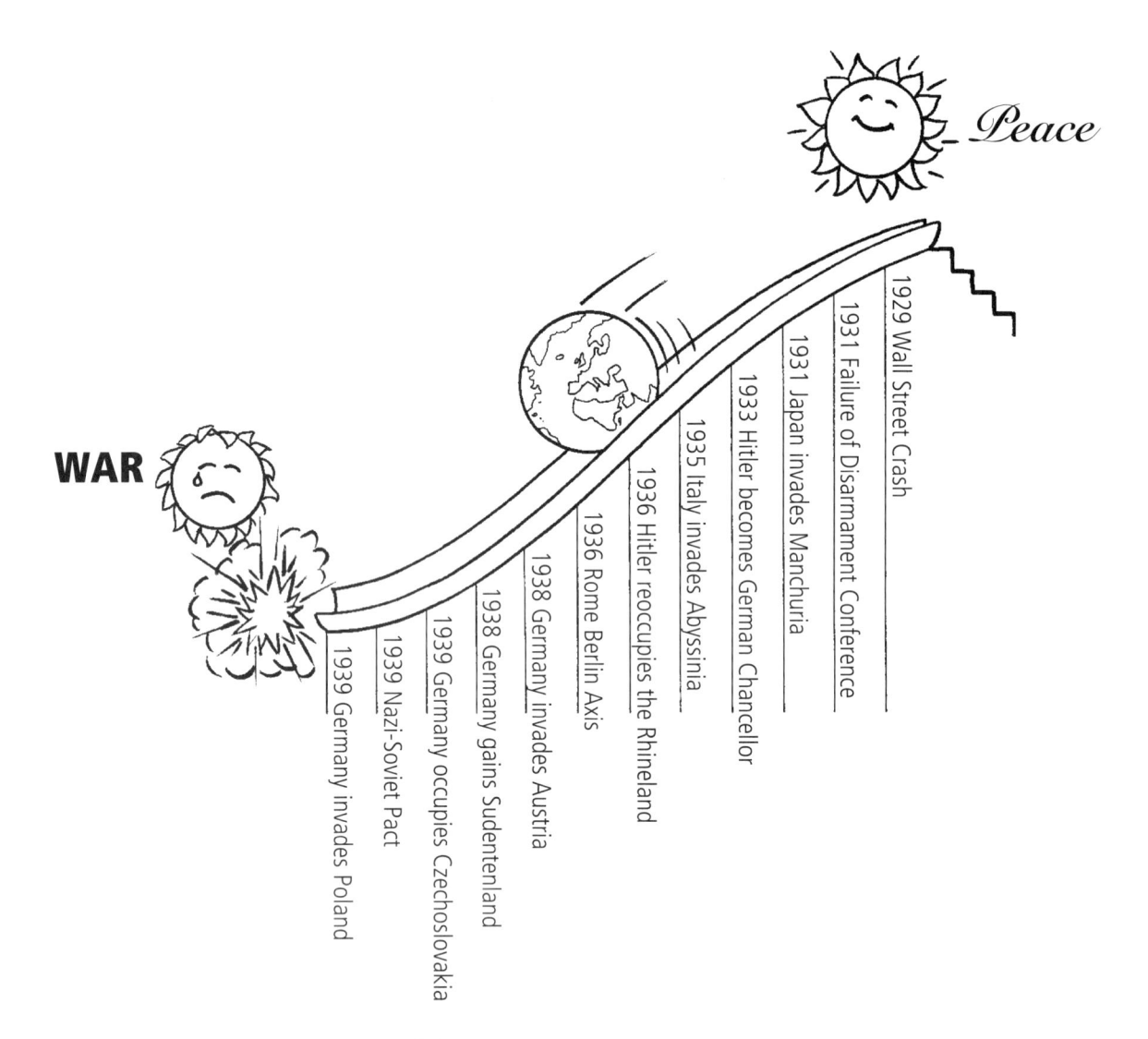

- 1929 Wall Street Crash
- 1931 Failure of Disarmament Conference
- 1931 Japan invades Manchuria
- 1933 Hitler becomes German Chancellor
- 1935 Italy invades Abyssinia
- 1936 Hitler reoccupies the Rhineland
- 1936 Rome Berlin Axis
- 1938 Germany invades Austria
- 1938 Germany gains Sudentenland
- 1939 Germany occupies Czechoslovakia
- 1939 Nazi-Soviet Pact
- 1939 Germany invades Poland

▲ The slide to war.

So had the policy of appeasement been justified?

Chamberlain had attempted to prevent war by giving in to Hitler's demands. In 1938 this policy appeared to be working, but by the end of 1939 it had been shown to be unsuccessful. Was it justified? Obviously this is a question you will need to answer yourself, but here are some suggestions to help you.

Against:

- Appeasement was morally wrong. If Hitler was using 'bullying' tactics it was up to Britain to oppose him.
- By following appeasement Britain betrayed the Austrians and the Czechs.
- Appeasement just made Britain look weak and gave Hitler the confidence to step up his demands.
- Appeasement did not work because Hitler could not be trusted to keep his word.

For:

- Britain was not ready to go to war and had to buy time to prepare.
- Germany was mistreated at Versailles and most of Hitler's demands were reasonable.
- War had to be avoided at all costs.
- Hitler was anti-communist and was doing a good job of restoring Germany – so he should be supported.
- By following the policy of appeasement Hitler was shown to be clearly in the wrong and a man who could not trusted – so the British people would not hesitate to go to war.

Summary box 4

For appeasement	Against appeasement
Britain not strong enough for war	Appeasement made Britain look weak
Germany mistreated at Versailles	Appeasement betrayed Austria and Czechoslovakia
Hitler was bringing stability to Germany	Hitler was given increased confidence
War had to be avoided	Hitler could not be trusted
Hitler clearly seen as the aggressor	

Road to War, 1929–39

3. What do I Know?

Once you have revised this topic thoroughly you should be able to answer most of these questions without using your notes. How many can you get right?

1. Who owned Manchuria in 1932?
2. What did the Japanese call Manchuria after they captured it?
3. Who ruled Abyssinia in 1935?
4. Which agreement in 1935 offered Mussolini two-thirds of Abyssinia?
5. Which agreement was signed by Italy and Germany in 1936?
6. What did Hitler think of the Treaty of Versailles?
7. When did Germany leave the League of Nations?
8. What did some politicians describe as Hitler 'marching into his own backyard'?
9. Where did the Luftwaffe gain valuable experience in war?
10. Give one reason why some British politicians thought that Hitler should be supported.
11. Which British prime minister followed the policy of appeasement?
12. Which British politician thought that appeasement was the same as showing weakness?
13. What was Anschluss?
14. What did Chamberlain say he had achieved at Munich?
15. Which country was doomed when the Nazi-Soviet Pact was signed?

My score ………

What was important about:
- The Treaty of Versailles
- The Japanese invasion of Manchuria
- The Hoare-Laval Pact
- The Munich Conference
- The Nazi-Soviet Pact?

4. Exam Type Question

A common exam question is one about the causes of the war. Here is an example.

'The Second World War broke out solely because of Hitler's aggressive foreign policy.' Do you agree **(20 marks)**

Answer 1

I agree with this statement. Hitler came to power in Germany in 1933 and soon began rearming. He took Germany out of the League of Nations, built up its armed forces and reintroduced conscription. He soon took over the Saar coalfields and put German troops back into the Rhineland – even though this had been banned in the Treaty of Versailles.

He reached an agreement with Mussolini which gave him the confidence to push on with his aggression. He sent troops to the Spanish Civil War and in 1937 took over Austria. Then in 1938 he bullied the Czechs into handing over the Sudentenland. Despite promising that he did not want any more territory he took over the rest of Czechoslovakia and finally in September 1939 invaded Poland. It is obvious that the war was his fault.

Road to War, 1929–39

Answer 2

> I don't think this is true. Certainly Hitler was a major cause of the Second World War, but there were other reasons too. The Germans were so badly treated at Versailles that another war was bound to happen; the League of Nations was too weak to keep peace; and Britain's policy of appeasement also gave Hitler the confidence to keep making demands. And then there is the Nazi-Soviet Pact. Without that there might not have been a war.
>
> Hitler was definitely a major reason why war broke out. He built Germany up to be a major military power and wasn't frightened to use that power to get his own way. He re-militarised the Rhineland and occupied Austria. Then he forced the Czechs to give him the Sudentenland. He did not seem to care that he was breaking the Treaty of Versailles. When he invaded Poland in September 1939 Britain and France declared war.
>
> Of course Hitler would not have been so successful if the people of Germany had been less resentful of the Treaty of Versailles. In that treaty the Germans were told that the war was all their fault and land was taken from them. Germany was even split in two. The Germans were bound to fight a war of revenge as soon as they were strong enough.
>
> The League also has to take some blame. What is the point of a peace-keeping organisation that doesn't do anything? Once the League acted so weakly against Japan and Italy everyone knew that it could not stop war and was nothing to be frightened of. Britain's role was not too impressive either. It's policy of appeasement just made Hitler think that he could get whatever he wanted.
>
> So there were lots of causes of the Second World War.

Examiner's Comments: Answer 1

The amount of historical knowledge in this answer is impressive and certainly shows that Hitler was to blame for the war. What it does not do, however, is to consider whether Hitler was solely to blame. It has missed out all the other factors, so can't really score any more than 8 marks.

Answer 2

This is a good essay. It shows an understanding of the need to look at other factors apart from Hitler and is generally supported with historical detail. The section on appeasement is disappointing with no facts to back up the argument, but the answer would still be worth 15 marks. With more facts it would have scored even higher.

5. Second World War, 1939-45

1. Topic Summary

In 1939 Europe went to war. Within a year Britain 'stood alone' against the Axis powers, Germany and Italy. However, during 1941 Britain's fortunes took a turn for the better. In June 1941 Hitler invaded the Soviet Union and began a campaign which was to prove a major drain on his resources. In December 1941 the Japanese bombed Pearl Harbor and brought America into the war. From mid-1942 onwards the course of the war changed as the Allies moved slowly, but surely, towards victory.

2. What do I Need to Know?

The most commonly asked questions on the war are why the Germans were defeated and why Japanese success in the Pacific was so short-lived. You will also need to explain the differences between this war and the First World War and to consider specific issues, such as why the British didn't make peace in 1940 and whether the Americans were justified in dropping the atomic bomb on Japan. You will need to know about the effects of the war on civilians, especially on women, and the effects of bombing.

3. History of the War

The war against Germany: Western Europe, 1939-41

- In September 1939 German forces swept into Poland and using blitzkrieg tactics quickly conquered the country.
- Britain prepared for war but from September until April there was a phoney war.
- In April 1940 the Germans invaded Norway and Denmark. Then, in May, they launched Operation Yellow and invaded France, Belgium, Luxembourg and Holland.
- The British troops in France helping the French were pushed back and had to be rescued from the beaches at Dunkirk.
- The French surrendered. Northern France came under German rule, but southern France was governed from Vichy by General Petain.
- Hitler now launched his attack on the British air force in the Battle of Britain, but could not defeat the RAF.
- In September 1940 he changed tactics and decided to bomb the British into submission. This was the Blitz, which lasted until May 1941.

Summary box 1

The war in Western Europe, 1939–41
- Blitzkrieg in Poland
- Phoney war
- Operation Yellow and defeat of France
- Battle of Britain
- The Blitz

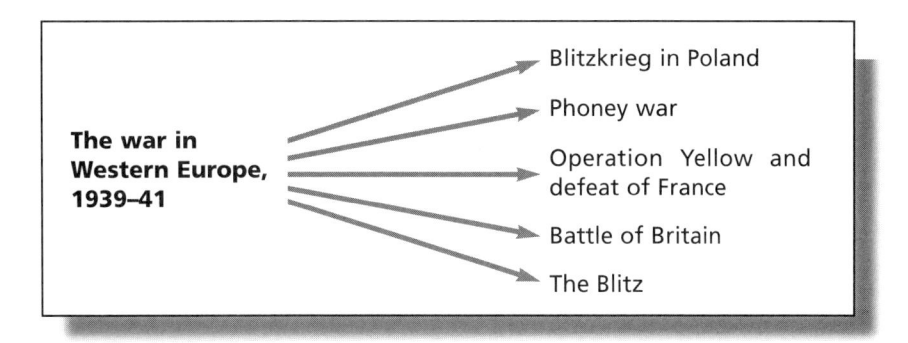

The war against Germany and Italy: Africa and the Soviet Union, 1940–3

- In September 1940 Hitler's ally Mussolini launched an attack on Egypt, a British colony.
- The Italians were easily defeated, but the Germans sent troops under Rommel who soon pushed the British and Empire forces back.
- In October 1942 Montgomery defeated Rommel's troops at El Alamein.
- In November 1942 American troops led by Eisenhower arrived in North Africa. By May 1943 they had helped the British defeat the Germans.
- In June 1941 Hitler invaded the Soviet Union. His troops advanced quickly and were soon at the gates of Moscow.
- However, the Soviets used a scorched earth policy and when winter came the German advance came to a halt.
- German losses were very heavy, both in fighting and from the cold, but by the spring of 1942 they were threatening two of the Soviet Union's main cities, Stalingrad and Leningrad.

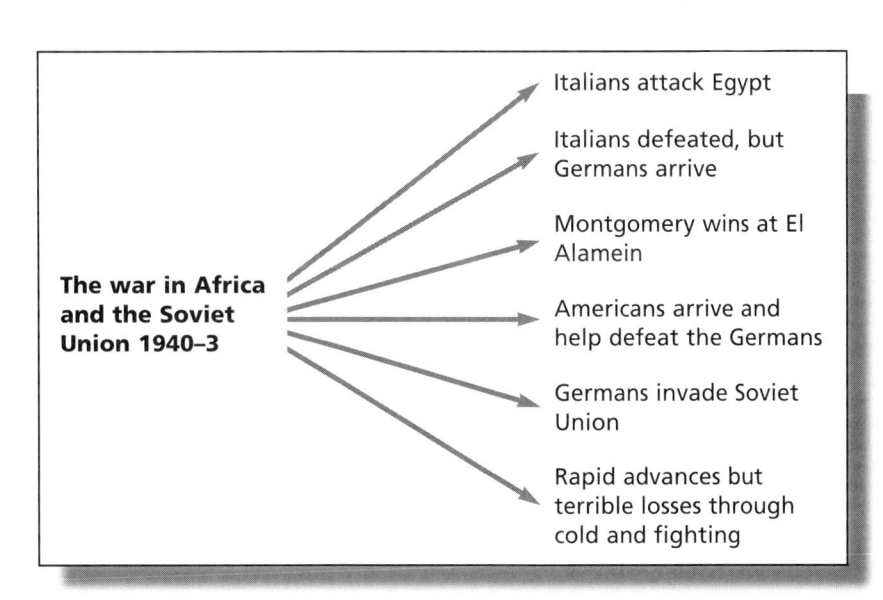

Summary box 2

The war in Africa and the Soviet Union 1940–3
- Italians attack Egypt
- Italians defeated, but Germans arrive
- Montgomery wins at El Alamein
- Americans arrive and help defeat the Germans
- Germans invade Soviet Union
- Rapid advances but terrible losses through cold and fighting

The war against Japan, 1941–2

- During the 1930s the Japanese tried to set up the Greater East Asia Co-Prosperity Sphere.
- The Americans in particular objected to Japanese expansion and imposed trade sanctions.
- By 1941 the Japanese had decided to gain land in the Pacific by force. They knew that Britain, France and Holland could not stop them, but were worried what the Americans would do.
- So in December 1941 the attacked the US Pacific fleet at Pearl Harbor and sank eight battleships.
- Then they went on the attack in South-East Asia and by mid-1942 were in control of almost the whole area, including Malaya, the Philippines and Singapore.

Summary box 3

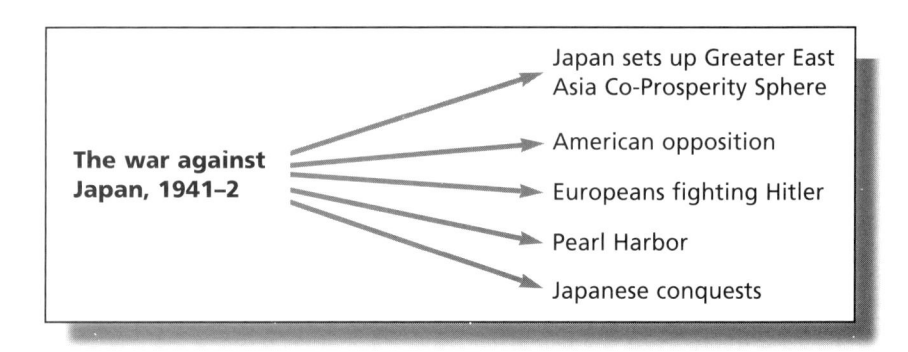

The war against Japan, 1941–2
- Japan sets up Greater East Asia Co-Prosperity Sphere
- American opposition
- Europeans fighting Hitler
- Pearl Harbor
- Japanese conquests

The defeat of Germany and Italy, 1943–5

- In mid-1943 Germany was in control of almost all of Europe, but its position was not as strong as it looked.
- In the Soviet Union enormous resources were being used up trying to win victory. After a heavy defeat at Stalingrad, the German commander, Von Paulus, surrendered in January 1943. The Soviet campaign had cost almost 250,000 German lives.
- As the Germans surrendered, so Soviet troops advanced westwards and by the end of 1944 were crossing the borders of Germany.
- In July 1943 Allied forces left Africa and landed in Sicily. They began advancing through Italy and by April 1945 had full control of the country. Mussolini was shot by Italian freedom fighters.
- On 6 June 1944 (D-Day) Allied forces landed in Normandy and began the long advance to Germany. In April 1945 they reached Berlin, where they met Soviet forces which had advanced from the east.
- Germany also faced attacks from the skies. British and American bombers carried out massive raids which caused terrible destruction in German cities.
- On 30 April 1945 Hitler committed suicide and Admiral Doenitz surrendered to the Allies on 7 May.

Second World War, 1939–45

Summary box 4

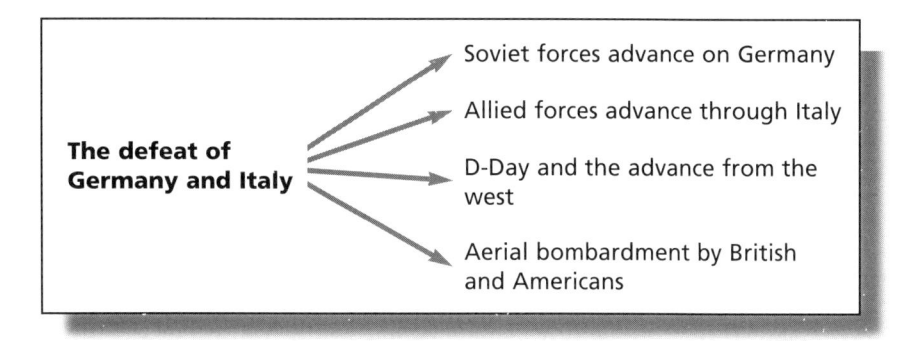

The defeat of Germany and Italy
- Soviet forces advance on Germany
- Allied forces advance through Italy
- D-Day and the advance from the west
- Aerial bombardment by British and Americans

The defeat of Japan, 1942–5

- When Japan attacked Pearl Harbor it weakened the Americans and enabled the Japanese forces to make conquests.
- But by mid-1942 the Americans had recovered and began to win victories at sea, such as at Coral Sea and Midway Island.
- Slowly all the Japanese gains were recovered by a process known as island hopping.
- In 1945 the Americans carried out massive bombing raids on Japan, and in some attacks, such as that on Tokyo in March, thousands of Japanese civilians were killed.
- At the end of July 1945 the Japanese asked the Soviet Union to try to negotiate a surrender which included allowing them to keep their emperor.
- America's President Truman said the surrender had to be unconditional, so the Japanese fought on – even when they were threatened with the atomic bomb.
- Truman was not prepared to suffer the huge losses that would result from an invasion of Japan so he agreed to the use of the atomic bomb. On 6 August 1945 a bomb was dropped on Hiroshima, causing 80,000 deaths. Three days later a second bomb was dropped on Nagasaki, causing another 40,000 deaths.
- Japan then surrendered. It had lost over one million soldiers and 600,000 civilians.

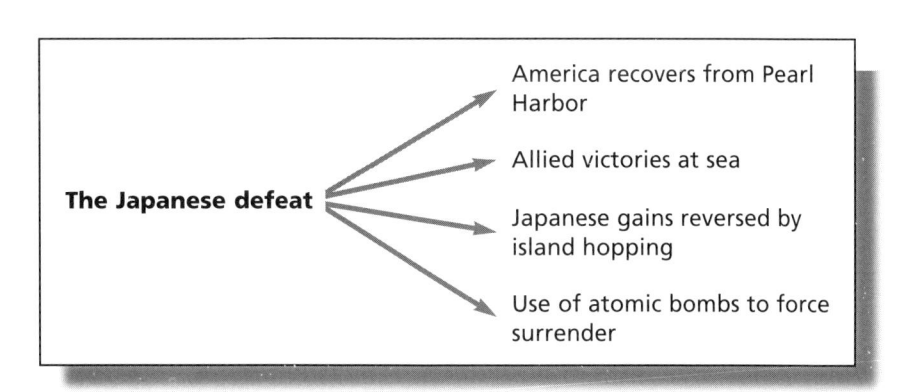

Summary box 5

The Japanese defeat
- America recovers from Pearl Harbor
- Allied victories at sea
- Japanese gains reversed by island hopping
- Use of atomic bombs to force surrender

Should the Americans have dropped the atomic bombs?

There is much argument between historians over this. Here are some of the points they make.

For:
- The Japanese were such fanatical fighters that thousands of Allied lives had been lost in recapturing territory. Hundreds of thousands would have died capturing Japan itself.
- The Japanese had been given the opportunity to surrender but had not done so.
- The Japanese had been warned of the consequences if they did not surrender.
- The war would be brought to a speedy conclusion.
- The Soviet Union would see how powerful the Americans were and so would be less likely to spread communism after the war.

Against:
- Japan was close to defeat. Continued blockades and bombing would finish the job.
- Mass killing of civilians could not be justified.
- Once the atomic bomb was used in warfare, then the very existence of the human race might be threatened.
- It was just America showing how strong it was.

Why did the Allies win the war?

- British determination. Although Britain stood alone in mid-1940 it would not surrender. Much of the credit for this should go to Winston Churchill for his inspirational leadership.
- Germany's invasion of the Soviet Union. German forces were to be involved in fierce fighting and suffered terrible losses.
- The Japanese attack on Pearl Harbor. This brought America into the war with its enormous resources supplying the Allies.
- Air and sea supremacy. By the end of the war both Germany and Japan were being strangled by naval blockades and bombed continuously from the air.
- The development of the atomic bomb. Once America decided to use this bomb, Japan stood no chance.
- The heroic resistance put up by the Russians seriously weakened the Germans.

Civilians and the war

The Second World War had a major impact on civilian life and led to huge casualties. For example, 20 million Soviet citizens died (which was more than the total deaths in the First World War).

- Civilians suffered from bombing raids during the war and the restrictions that went with them, such as blackouts and evacuation.
- The war also caused food shortages and rationing.
- Civilians were forced to join their country's armed forces (conscription).
- Many countries suffered occupation by foreign forces. The Japanese were particularly harsh in their treatment of foreign civilians. The Germans used civilians from conquered countries in eastern Europe as slave labour. They also carried out an

extermination campaign (the Holocaust) against the Jewish race and against Slavs in the Soviet Union.
- In most occupied countries resistance groups were formed who carried out secret operations against their conquerors. The most famous of these was the Maquis (the French resistance).
- Civilians were also subjected to mass propaganda to convince them that their country was in the right.

How was the Second World War different to the First World War?

Some of the major differences were:
- The Second World War was based much more on technology, e.g. fighter planes and bombers, paratroopers, tanks, aircraft carriers, radar, the atomic bomb.
- As a result the war was much more mobile than the First. Much of the fighting in 1914–18 had been done in trenches, where there was stalemate. German blitzkrieg tactics made the Second World War very different.
- The early involvement of America and Japan made the Second World War more widespread and more sea-based. Between 1942 and 1945 there were sea battles involving huge aircraft carriers.
- The Second World War had a much greater impact on civilians. In the 1914–18 war there was conscription, food shortages and bombing, but in the 1939–45 war the impact was so much greater because of improved technology. So, huge numbers of civilians died in bombing raids. And millions died in the Holocaust.
- Women in Britain were involved in a wider role than in the First World War. Some were involved in all three armed forces.

What do I Know?

Once you have revised this topic thoroughly you should be able to answer most of these questions without using your notes. How many can you get right?

1. What tactics did Germany use to defeat Poland?
2. From where were British troops rescued in 1940?
3. What was the Blitz?
4. Where did Montgomery defeat Rommel in 1942?
5. What is a 'scorched earth policy'?
6. How many men did the Germans lose in the Soviet Union?
7. Where did the Japanese bomb in December 1941?
8. What name was given to the German genocide against the Jews?
9. When was 'D-Day'?
10. What was 'island hopping'?
11. Name one major sea defeat suffered by the Japanese.
12. Where did the Americans drop the first atomic bomb?
13. What happened to Mussolini in April 1945?
14. What happened to Hitler in April 1945?
15. Who were the Maquis?

My score ………

What was important about:
- Blitzkrieg
- The Battle of Britain
- Pearl Harbor
- The dropping of the atomic bomb
- Technological change?

Second World War, 1939–45

5. Exam Type Questions

Look carefully at Sources A and B. One of these sources was produced in the First World War and one was produced in the Second World War. Which war do you think each one came from? Use your knowledge to explain your answer. **(10 marks)**

Source A

A Call from the Trenches.

(Extract from a letter from the Trenches.)

"I SAW a recruiting advertisement in a paper the other day. I wonder if the men are responding properly —they would if they could see what the Germans have done in Belgium. And, after all, it's not so bad out here—cold sometimes, and the waiting gets on our nerves a bit, but we are happy and as fit as fiddles. I wonder if———has joined, he certainly ought to."

Does "———" refer to you?

If so

ENLIST TO-DAY.

God Save the King.

◀ This advertisement for recruits for the war appeared in *The Times*.

Source B

DON'T do it, Mother—
LEAVE THE CHILDREN WHERE THEY ARE

ISSUED BY THE MINISTRY OF HEALTH

◀ This government war poster warned parents of the danger to their children if they stayed in the cities.

Answer 1

I think that Source A comes from the First World War because it talks about trenches and Source B is from the Second World War because it has Hitler in it.

Answer 2

Obviously Source A is from the First World War because it talks about the trenches, which is where most of the fighting was done – on the Western Front. It also talks about Belgium, which is where the Germans invaded to bring Britain into the war. I expect there were some trenches in the Second World War, but improved technology meant that tanks and planes could deal with trenches very easily, which they could not do in the First World War.

The article is really a recruiting advertisement and is using guilt to get people to join up. This is another reason why I know it's from the First World War. To start with the British relied on volunteers to fight the Germans. From 1916 they introduced conscription, which they also had during all the Second World War, so they didn't need to have these sorts of articles.

Source B has Hitler in it and is designed to show people that evacuation is a good thing so Hitler would oppose it. So this must be from the Second World War.

Examiner's Comments on: Answer 1

Although this answer is correct it could not expect to score high marks. There are ten marks for this question and the candidate was asked to use knowledge to explain. You won't get many marks out of 10 for a three line answer. I would not give this more than 3 marks.

Answer 2

This answer is extremely good on Source A where it tells us why the source must be from the First World War and cannot be from the Second World War. That is a much better approach than just saying that it comes from one of them. Source B, however, is not handled quite so well and needs details of why a poster promoting evacuation would not come from the First World War. I would give this answer 8 marks.

Practice Question

Now answer the question yourself. Look at answer 2 and see what you would need to add to get the extra two marks.

Germany, 1918–45

6. Weimar Republic, 1918–33

1. Topic Summary

The Weimar Republic was established in November 1918, just two days before Germany surrendered at the end of the First World War. Defeat in the war was the first of a series of problems that would hinder the new government. The Republic dealt with it's initial problems and after 1923 it seemed to be creating a wealthy and vibrant Germany. Unfortunately the Wall Street Crash stirred the old hatreds. The Republic was soon in serious trouble and did not last beyond 1933.

2. What do I Need to Know?

You will need to know the different problems facing the new Republic in 1919 and to understand the instability that existed in Germany up to 1923. You will also need to appreciate the problems created by hyperinflation. However, you must not see this as leading to the inevitable end of the Republic. The years 1923-9 were prosperous and vibrant for many Germans.

3. History of the Weimar Republic

The Treaty of Versailles

The treaty had a major impact on Germans. It is vital you learn what it's terms were, and how these affected Germany's foreign and domestic policies.

- Germany was to pay for all the deaths and damage that had been caused by fighting.
- Germany lost its colonies, 13 per cent of its land and 6 million people. The country was split in two.
- Germany's army was reduced to just 100,000 men; it was left with six battleships; and it was not allowed to have an air force. No military activity was allowed in the Rhineland.
- Under Article 231 Germany accepted all responsibility for starting the war. This gave the Allies the legal right to punish Germany.

Reactions to the Treaty

- Many Germans felt betrayed by the treaty. They accused politicians of stabbing the army in the back. It soon became accepted as 'fact' that the army would have won the war if the politicians of the Republic had not given up.

- Germans felt ashamed that they were forced to accept the blame for the war.
- Many Germans were so resentful over what had happened that they demanded that when the country was strong enough it should gain revenge.

Summary box 1

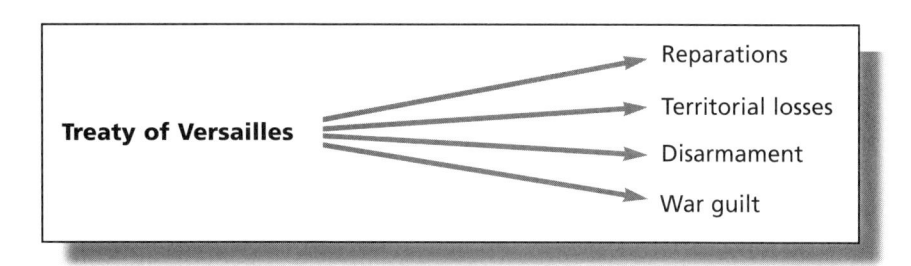

Treaty of Versailles
- Reparations
- Territorial losses
- Disarmament
- War guilt

Early problems for the Republic

Political challenges

The Weimar Republic was not popular among Germans and there were several attempts to overthrow it. Where did the main challenges come from?

- There were left-wing uprisings in:
  - Bavaria (1919). An attempted communist uprising was later crushed.
  - Berlin (1919). The Spartacist uprising led by Rosa Luxembourg and Karl Liebknecht was put down and the two leaders shot.

- There were right-wing rebellions in:
  - Berlin (1920), led by Kapp, who later fled and committed suicide.
  - Munich (1923), led by Hitler, who was arrested and imprisoned.

- Political extremism
  - Four main parties opposed the Republic: Communists, Independent Socialists, Nationalists and Nazis.
  - When the Republic got into trouble, people voted for the Communists and Nazis because they promised to take decisive action.
  - Erzberger and Rathenau, two leading Weimar politicians, were both assassinated.

Voting system

The Republic also faced problems because of its voting system. It used proportional representation, which meant that even small political parties could get some representatives elected to the Reichstag. No one party had a majority in the Reichstag and so coalitions had to be formed. Those making up the coalitions often fell out among themselves.

Political system of the Weimar Republic	
Voting rights	Under the Weimar constitution, every adult (male and female) aged 20 or over could vote in the elections.
The Reichstag	Every four years the people of Germany would vote for a political party. These votes would be counted and used to decide how many seats each party would receive. If 20 per cent of voters voted for the Nazis, they received 20 per cent of the seats. (This is called proportional representation.) Usually the party with the largest number of seats had its leader as Chancellor (Prime Minister).
The President	Every seven years an election would be held for President. The President was really just a figurehead, though he did choose the Chancellor. He also could take emergency powers under Article 48 of the Constitution.

Summary box 2

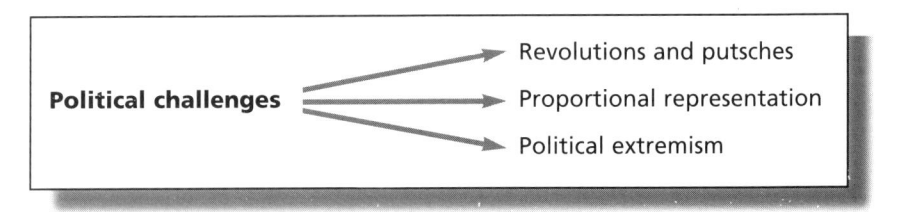

Political challenges
- Revolutions and putsches
- Proportional representation
- Political extremism

Economic problems

After the war the German economy was in ruins, but slowly it began to recover. Then the German government was told it had to pay £6,600 million to the Allies as reparations for the war. After one year it defaulted on the payments. The French were so angry that they seized the Ruhr area, Germany's main industrial region. German workers went on strike and the economy collapsed into inflation.

Hyperinflation

Inflation is when the price of goods goes up periodically. Hyperinflation is much, much worse. Prices do not just go up periodically; they rise rapidly and out of control. Wages cannot keep up with price increases.

In Germany, the price of goods just spiralled out of control. For example, in 1918 a loaf of bread cost 0.63 marks; in January 1923 it cost 250 marks; in November 1923 it cost 201,000,000,000 marks.

Causes of hyperinflation:
- Germany had to pay back the money it borrowed to pay for the First World War.

- Reparations. Germany could not afford to pay the money due.
- The government printed too much money. Money became worthless.
- The French and Belgians invaded the Ruhr. Germany lost an important industrial area.

Winners from hyperinflation:
- Landowners. Even in times of major crisis land is a symbol of wealth. As prices went up so did the value of land.
- Borrowers. If you borrowed a million marks in 1919 it was a great deal of money. By 1923, it was worthless and you could pay it back easily.
- Big businesses. They were able to sell their goods abroad in exchange for valuable currencies.

Losers from hyperinflation:
- Savers. In 1919 5,000 marks was a fortune. By 1923, it would not buy a stamp for a letter ! Those with life savings in a bank found that the money was worthless.
- Small businesses. They could not deal with huge amounts of money or raising their prices every hour.
- Lenders. They could never recover the lost money.
- Pensioners. In 1919 a pension of 50 marks a week meant you were well off. By 1923 it bought nothing, so you were ruined.

The losers from hyperinflation blamed the Republic for the problems. This hatred of the government died down in the mid-1920s as Germany's economic problems were solved, only to return as world recession set in during the late 1920s and early 1930s.

Summary box 3

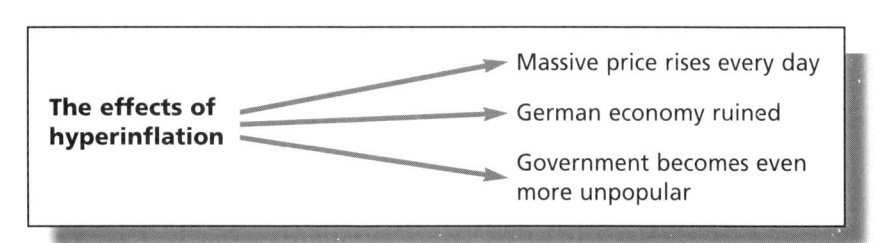

The effects of hyperinflation
- Massive price rises every day
- German economy ruined
- Government becomes even more unpopular

Munich Putsch

The Weimar Republic's problems made it so unpopular that there were attempts to overthrow it. One of these was led by Adolf Hitler.

- On 8 November 1923 Hitler entered a Munich beer hall in which the three leaders of Bavaria were speaking. Hitler declared himself President of Germany.
- The next day Hitler and his supporters marched on Munich.
- The state police and army held firm, and Hitler was arrested.

- Hitler's trial was a farce. During it he was allowed to make speech after speech denouncing all the groups he hated, especially the Weimar Republic, Jews and Communists. Hitler came across as a hero when he declared that Germany had been betrayed in the Treaty of Versailles and that it should be torn up.
- He received a sentence of five years but served only nine months. During this period he dictated his book *Mein Kampf*. In it he set out his beliefs.

Summary box 4

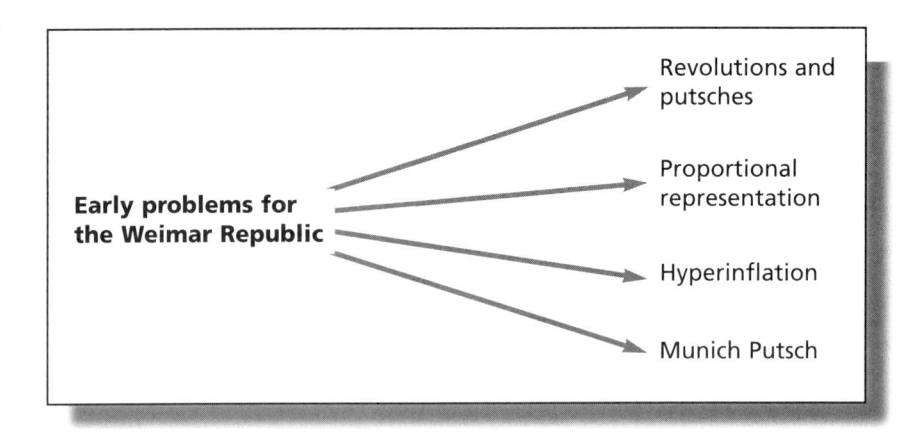

Early problems for the Weimar Republic:
- Revolutions and putsches
- Proportional representation
- Hyperinflation
- Munich Putsch

Stresemann

From late 1923 the Weimar Republic recovered, largely due to the work of Gustav Stresemann. He introduced measures which restored the German economy and relations with other countries.

- He solved hyperinflation with the introduction of a new currency, the Rentenmark. This replaced the old currency and brought back confidence and stability.
- He solved the economic problems by arranging loans from America under the Dawes Plan in which new terms for the payment of reparations was set out. This provided the backing for the new currency. It created prosperity.
- He solved the problem of the Ruhr by resuming the reparation payments. The French now left. This impressed the German people, who wanted the French out of Germany.

Stresemann after 1923

- The Young Plan of 1929 carried on the work of the Dawes Plan by extending the reparation payments by a further 59 years. Germany was starting to sort out it's economy.
- Relations with other countries were improved by signing the Locarno and Kellogg-Briand Pacts. Germany joined the League of Nations in 1926. It was now part of the family of nations.
- This period saw developments in the arts. The Bauhaus style of architecture was trend-setting, as was the film industry, with stars such as Marlene Dietrich.

But:

- Many people were concerned that Germany's prosperity was based on loans from abroad, especially from America.
- Despite the prosperity, helped by the American loans, the German government was spending too much on welfare benefits to the unemployed.

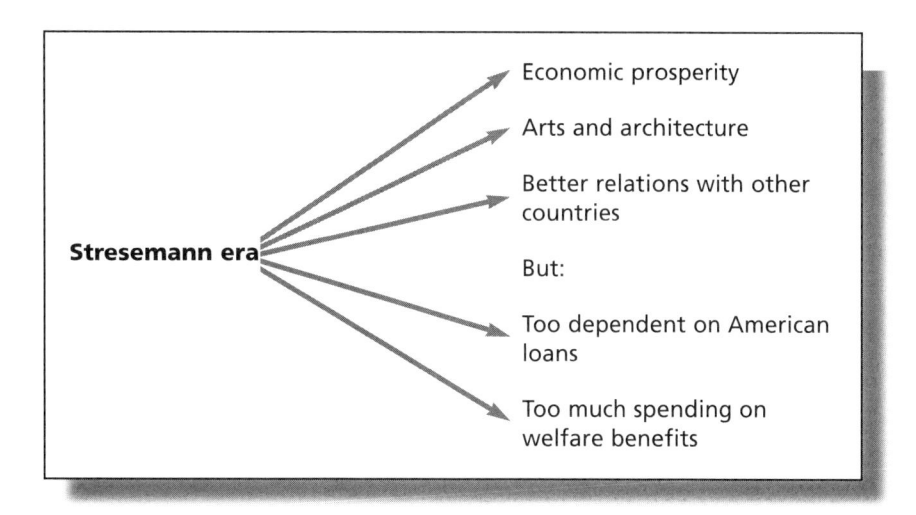

Summary box 5

Stresemann era:
- Economic prosperity
- Arts and architecture
- Better relations with other countries

But:
- Too dependent on American loans
- Too much spending on welfare benefits

Task 1 Copy the chart below and complete it to show the terms of the Treaty of Versailles.

Military

Army: _____ men

_____: 6 battleships

Airforce: ___ planes

Demilitarised _____

Land

Split into _____

Lost about 13% of _____

Lost all _____

No union with _____ allowed

Treaty of Versailles

Economic

Forced to pay £6,600 million in _____

Blame

Article _____, also known as the _____ _____ clause

Weimar Republic, 1918-33

Task 2 Copy the chart below and see if you can add arrows to show how the Dawes Plan was to help Germany.

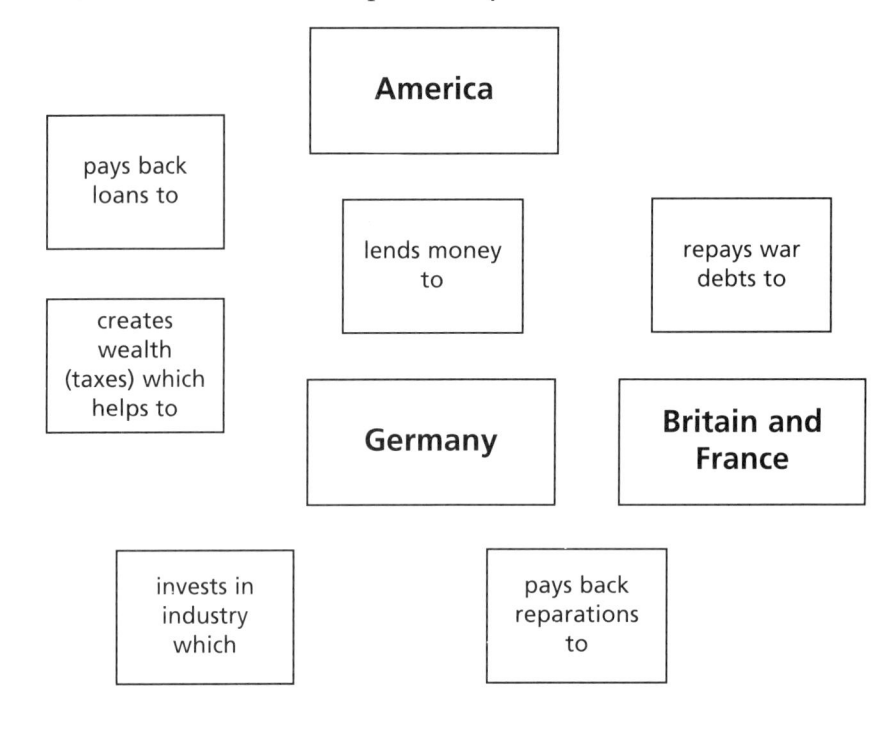

```
                    America
  pays back
  loans to
                 lends money        repays war
                    to              debts to

  creates
  wealth
  (taxes) which
  helps to         Germany         Britain and
                                     France

              invests in      pays back
              industry        reparations
              which           to
```

What do I Know?

Once you have revised this topic thoroughly you should be able to answer most of these questions without using your notes. How many can you get right?

1. When did fighting in the First World War cease?
2. Name the treaty that ended the First World War
3. What was Article 231 of the Treaty of Versailles better known as?
4. How many soldiers was the German army limited to?
5. Who were the Sparticists?
6. What did Kapp do?
7. Name one of the two countries that invaded the Ruhr in 1923?
8. In which year was the Munich Putsch?
9. Why did some people think Hitler's trial was a 'farce'?
10. What does 'Mein Kampf' mean?
11. Name one group that gained from hyperinflation.
12. Name one group that lost from hyperinflation.
13. What was the name of the new currency introduced by Stresemann?
14. What was the name of the plan in 1924 by which America lent Germany money?
15. When did Germany join the League of Nations?

My score ………

What was important about:
- The November Criminals
- Putsches
- Hyperinflation
- Stresemann?

Weimar Republic, 1918-33

5

Key Dates to Learn

1918	11 November	Armistice declared. End of war
1919	5–12 January	Spartacist uprisings in Berlin
	28 June	Treaty of Versailles signed
1920	13–17 March	Kapp Putsch
1923	January	Invasion of the Ruhr by French and Belgians
	August	Stresemann becomes Chancellor
	8–9 November	Hitler's 'Beer hall' Putsch in Munich
1924		Dawes Plan
1926	September	Germany joins League of Nations.

6

Using the Source

Study this cartoon about the Treaty of Versailles. Then answer the questions below.

"PERHAPS IT WOULD GEE-UP BETTER IF WE LET IT TOUCH EARTH"

▲ A British cartoon showing different reactions to the reparations imposed on Germany after the war.

1. Look at how the horse is sweating, yet cannot go forward. What does this mean?
2. Look how angry Briand is, and how puzzled Lloyd George looks. Why is this?
3. What does this cartoon tell us about the problems caused by reparations for the German government?
4. Do you think the cartoonist supported the idea of making Germany pay reparations? Explain your answer.

7. Exam Type Questions

Often in exams you are asked to assess the reliability of sources. Study the sources below and then answer the questions which follow.

Source A

> Vengeance, German nation! Today in the Hall of Mirrors the disgraceful treaty is being signed. Do not forget it. The German people will, with unceasing labour, press forward to reconquer the place amongst nations to which it is entitled. Then will come vengeance for the shame of 1919.

▲ An extract from a German newspaper.

Source B

> So it had all been in vain ... the death of two million. Had they died for this, so that a gang of wretched criminals could lay hands on the Fatherland?

▲ An extract from *Mein Kampf* (1925) written by Hitler. In it he is describing how German soldiers died in vain in the First World War.

Source C

> Hitler had been walking arm-in-arm with one of his colleagues. He was dragged to the ground with a dislocated shoulder when his colleague was shot and crumpled under the hail of lead. Hitler's bodyguard threw himself on his master, covering him with his body, so that he was safe.

▲ A description of the Munich Putsch from *I Knew Hitler* (1938) by Karl Ludecke.

Source D

> The body of the man with whom Hitler was linked shot up into the air like a ball, tearing Hitler's arm with him, so that it sprang from the joint and fell back limp and useless. Hitler realised that the 'man' was just a boy and that he was severely wounded. He picked him up and carried him on his shoulders. Suddenly a policeman recognised Hitler and took aim, but Hitler raised the boy above his head. He, at least, should live. The shot missed.

▲ From an official biography of Hitler.

Weimar Republic, 1918-33

> 1 How reliable are Sources A and B in studying German attitudes to the defeat in the war and the Treaty of Versailles? **(7 marks)**
>
> 2 How reliable are Sources C and D to an historian studying the events of the Munich Putsch? Explain your answer as fully as you can. **(7 marks)**

Question 1: Answer

Source A is unreliable because it is a newspaper, and all newspapers lie! Obviously Source B is unreliable because it is written by Hitler, and he is bound to be distorting the truth.

Examiner's Comments

The first stage in looking at reliability involves looking at: **who** wrote/said the source; **when** they wrote/said the source; and **why** they wrote/said the source.

Source A was written the day after the signing of the Treaty of Versailles. All Germans would have felt a similar sense of betrayal. The paper does not intend to be balanced in its viewpoint. Its readers would expect the paper to oppose the Treaty. So it is giving an exaggerated view, but it is saying what many Germans thought and so is reliable for giving a view of what some German attitudes were.

Source B was written by Hitler in order that people were aware that he blamed the Weimar Republic for Germany's defeat in the First World War. Hitler was opposed to the Republic and wished to replace it; obviously he would write bad things about it. But his statement is reliable for telling us what opponents of the Weimar Republic thought of the war and its consequences.

Another point to be aware of is the use of language. Both sources use emotive words, such as 'disgraceful' and 'wretched'. This is an obvious sign of bias, but it does not mean that what they are telling us is unreliable. What you have to do is check it against your knowledge of the period to see if it is reliable.

What this answer fails to do is look at *motivation*. Why did the authors say or write what they did? This is vital in looking at reliability. The answer makes judgements about both sources, but it does not attempt to back up those judgements by using either the historical context or the context of the sources. It would not score more than 1–2 marks.

Question 2: Answer 1

I think Sources C and D are not reliable because they are both written a long time after the event, and the writers have forgotten some of the important points or made some up of their own. The sources might be reliable if we found out information from eye-witnesses and they backed up the story. We need more information.

Weimar Republic, 1918-33

Answer 2

Of the two sources, Source D is obviously the least reliable. It was written in 1936 when Hitler was still in power and when no books were allowed that criticised him. This must have been written by a Nazi as it is an 'official' biography. The words used by the writer are obviously exaggerated. It is just not credible that a man with a dislocated shoulder could raise another human being above his head. It is intended to suggest that Hitler is a hero, a brave and strong man saving a boy. It's part of the propaganda used by the Nazis to win support.

Source C is not so simple. We would need to know more. Was the book written by a German in Germany or did they have to publish it abroad? In Germany the strict censorship laws were still in force in 1938. From my knowledge I know that some people died in the Putsch and that Hitler was injured, but this all sounds very dramatic. In order to more fully answer the question about this source I need to know a lot more about Ludecke and why he is writing about the event.

Examiner's Comments on: Answer 1

The answer fails to get to grips with reliability. It is a general answer and does not refer to the historical context at all. The first problem is that the answer links the two sources together rather than looking at each separately. It fails to consider the basic Who? When? Why? and it also fails to look at the content of the sources. Do not think that people writing about an event a long time after it took place automatically means they are distorting the facts or even telling lies. Actually being there does not make comments more reliable! This answer would get only 1–2 marks.

Answer 2

This answer tries to consider the aspects of Who? When? and Why? It also looks beyond the obvious and is analysing the language of the sources. It begins to suggest specific evidence that an historian might use to check out the sources. It has looked at each source separately and the student has used their knowledge of the period to consider the reliability of the sources. I would give 6–7 marks for this answer.

Practice Question

Now it is your turn. Re-read Sources C and D and answer question 2. Once you have written your answer compare it with the two above.

7. The Rise of Hitler

1. Topic Summary

In looking at the fall of the Weimar Republic, it is easy to say that Hitler was helped by the poverty and despair caused by the Depression. Connected with this idea is the one that if Stresemann had not died suddenly, then he may have been able to save the Republic. However, in history things are not quite so simple. Hitler was helped by the Depression, but he had spent the ten years after the Munich Putsch preparing for the opportunity to achieve power. Although Stresemann was a very able politician, it would seem even beyond his powers of persuasion to stop the American government and the banks demanding their money back.

2. What do I Need to Know?

You must be clear as to how the Depression affected Germany. You must also be aware of what it was that Hitler offered the German electorate that the politicians of the Republic could not or would not. You should also have an understanding of the role of Papen and Hindenburg in Hitler's rise to power. Then you will be expected to consider exactly why Hitler came to power.

3. History of Hitler's Rise to Power

Nazi beliefs

During the years 1924–9, Hitler had developed the Nazi Party's beliefs. This was contained in his Twenty-Five-Point programme. It stated that:

- **Race**. All things positive have been created by the Aryan people. Other races have a negative effect on society, and these must be isolated or removed.
- **Lebensraum**. As the master race, the Germans were entitled to lebensraum (living space) in the eastern part of Europe, and the Slavs living there would become slaves.
- **Anti-semitism**. Jews were 'parasites'. They made profits from the war; they were the 'November criminals'. They controlled the press, big business and the Republic.
- **One leader**. Hitler hated democracy. He believed in one leader who was not dependant upon pleasing the electors. He would make the difficult decisions. Under his leadership, all Germans would be united in a single Reich (Empire).
- **Treaty of Versailles**. This had been signed by 'criminals'. It must be ignored, with Germany's rightful possessions and people returned to it.

- **Anti–communism**. Hitler hated communism almost as much as he hated Jews. He saw it as a cancer that needed to be removed.
- **Strength**. Hitler believed that everything was gained by force. He believed in a strong army which would make Germany strong again.

Summary box 1

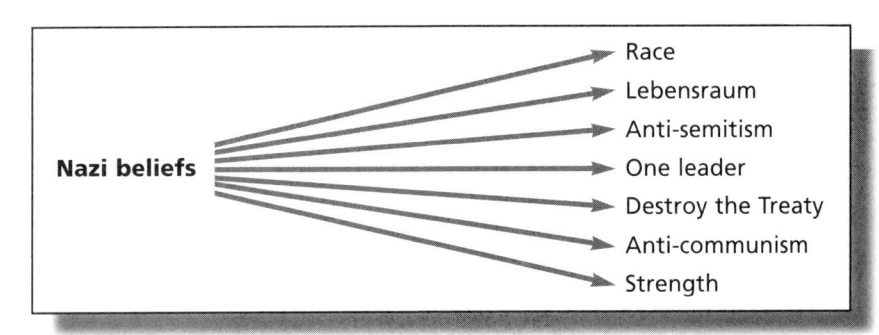

```
Nazi beliefs ──► Race
             ──► Lebensraum
             ──► Anti-semitism
             ──► One leader
             ──► Destroy the Treaty
             ──► Anti-communism
             ──► Strength
```

Supporters of Hitler

Hitler's different ideas appealed to many different groups.
- **Nationalists**. To those who thought that revising Germany's power was important, it was Hitler's nationalism that was stressed.
- **Racists**. For any one who was anti-semitic, it was Hitler's ideas on race that were emphasised.
- **Anti-communists**. The middle class and big business were attracted by his anti-communism. So were strongly religious people who saw communism as anti-religious.
- **Authoritarians**. To those who saw only chaos and had lost hope with democracy he emphasised his idea of the 'leader principle'; he would be in total control.
- **The unemployed**. The working class generally turned to the communists, but many were attracted to Hitler's calls for 'work and bread', particularly after the 1929 economic crash.
- **Women**. Eventually many women were attracted by the call to their loyalty to their families, that is, to vote for the Nazis in order to give their men a job.
- **The young**. Hitler developed support amongst the young even though they couldn't vote straight away. They would later on. The attraction was the parades, banners, the feeling of power, and that they would be part of a 'great Germany' in the future.

Summary box 2

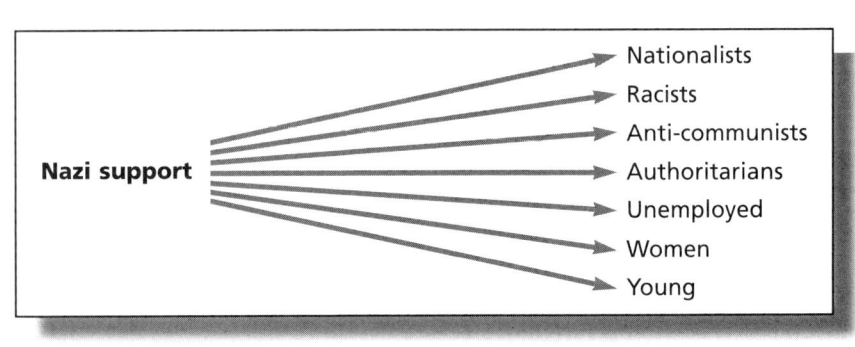

```
Nazi support ──► Nationalists
             ──► Racists
             ──► Anti-communists
             ──► Authoritarians
             ──► Unemployed
             ──► Women
             ──► Young
```

The stormtroopers

In order to deal with opposition to the Nazis and to whip up support at meetings and rallies, Hitler created a private army called the stormtroopers (or Brownshirts or SA). Anyone causing trouble at a Nazi rally or demonstrating against the Nazis in public was likely to be dealt with in a very forceful, physical way.

The Nazis, 1923–8

Despite the constant use of propaganda the Nazi Party made very little progress in the 1920s. Once Stresemann had helped solve Germany's problems the German people were much happier with the Republic. They had little time for extreme parties such as the Nazis. So in 1928 the Nazi Party won only 12 seats (out of over 400) in the elections to the Reichstag

The Depression

- In 1929, the Wall Street Crash in America forced American banks to recall their loans to Germany and German business.
- German industry was unable to cope with the fall in demand for their goods and was unable to pay back their loans. Millions of workers were made unemployed as factories closed.
- By 1933, unemployment figures had reached over 6 million. There were high levels of poverty and distress. The Republic seemed incapable of dealing with the problem.
- There were a series of coalition governments. The different parties could not agree on the correct policies. Some wished to cut benefits to save money. Others thought it would cause more misery.
- The only parties to gain from this were the Communists and the Nazis. While millions were left idle, these parties offered positive action.
- After 1929, the Chancellor was using the emergency powers of the President (Article 48) to rule the country.
- Chancellor Papen and President Hindenburg decided to invite Hitler to be Chancellor. They secretly believed they could control Hitler, and use his representatives in the Reichstag to support their policies.

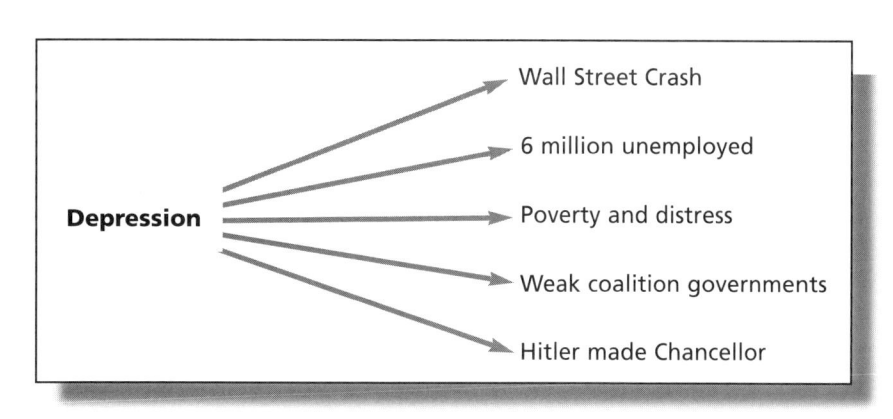

Summary box 3

Depression →
- Wall Street Crash
- 6 million unemployed
- Poverty and distress
- Weak coalition governments
- Hitler made Chancellor

The Rise of Hitler

Practice Task

Give one reason why each of the following people might have given the Nazis their support in the period after 1929:

- An upper-class general (retired)
- A middle-class shopkeeper
- A working-class labourer (unemployed).

Can you think of anything Hitler believed in which might have stopped these people supporting the Nazis? Remember not everyone is the same, even in the same class.

4 What do I Know?

Once you have revised this topic thoroughly you should be able to answer most of these questions without using your notes. How many can you get right?

1. Which race did Hitler think was the world's leading race?
2. What was lebensraum?
3. Who were the 'November criminals'?
4. Why did Hitler disapprove of democracy?
5. What is a 'Reich'?
6. Why did some people with religious convictions support the Nazis?
7. People who hate Jews are called what?
8. What was the name of the programme which stated the Nazi Party beliefs?
9. What event in America in 1929 harmed Germany?
10. Who was President of Germany in 1929?
11. What was the name of the special powers that the President could use to run the country?
12. Why was there such high unemployment in Germany in 1933?
13. How did high unemployment affect support for the Nazis?
15. What month and year did Hitler become Chancellor?
15. Who invited Hitler to become Chancellor?

My score ………

What is important about:

- Hitler's skills as a leader
- The Wall Street Crash
- Mass unemployment?

5 Key Dates to Learn

1923	13 August	August Stresemann becomes Chancellor
	8–9 November	Hitler's 'Beer hall' Putsch in Munich
1925	27 April	Hindenburg elected President
1926	September	Germany joins the League of Nations
1929	October–November	Wall Street Crash, start of the Depression
1932	10 April	Hindenburg re-elected as President, beating Hitler
1933	30 January	Hitler becomes Chancellor.

The Rise of Hitler

6 Exam Type Question

Study the sources A and B below. Is there enough information in the sources to explain why Hitler became Chancellor in 1933? Explain your answer fully. **(7 marks)**

Source A

Party (with initials)	1919	1920	1924 May	1924 Dec.	1928	1930	1932 July	1932 Nov.
National Socialist (Nazis)	–	–	32	14	12	107	230	196
National (DNVP)	44	71	95	103	73	41	37	52
People's (DVP)	19	65	45	51	45	30	7	11
Centre (Z)	91	64	65	69	62	68	75	70
Democratic (DDP)	75	39	28	32	25	20	4	2
Social Democrat (SPD)	165	102	100	131	153	143	133	121
Independent Socialist (USPD)	22	84	–	–	–	–	–	–
Communist (KPD)	–	4	62	45	54	77	89	100

▲ Results of elections for seats in the Reichstag, 1919–32.

Source B

Sept. 1928	Sept. 1929	Sept. 1930	Sept. 1931	Sept. 1932	Jan. 1933
650,000	1,320,000	3,000,000	4,350,000	5,102,000	6,100,000

▲ Unemployment figures in Germany, 1928–33.

Hints for answer

This is a common type of question in exams. To answer it you must:

1 State what the source(s) explains.
2 State what is missing from the source(s) or what is wrong. Revision is essential for this point.
3 You should suggest specific sources of information you could use to fill the gaps. You must not give a generalised 'more photographs, diaries and eye-witnesses' answer. Photographs of what? Whose diary? Which eye-witnesses and why?
4 Consider reliability. Have you got any reason to doubt the source?

The Rise of Hitler

Answer 1

> I don't think there is enough information in Sources A and B, because an historian can never get enough information. He would need to find out whether the statistics are true, as they could be made up. However if you look at Source B you can see that unemployment has risen, which I know is true, and I know lots of unemployed people did vote for Hitler, as he did offer 'bread and work'.

Answer 2

> Source A gives the number of members of the Reichstag between 1928 and 1932. However they are just figures. They do show that the Nazis became the largest party, but they don't show why. Source B gives a reason why the Nazis did so well. It shows the rise in unemployment, and Nazis promised 'bread and work' to the German people.
>
> The problem with both sources is that they do not show the other reasons why the Nazis were popular. They don't show the promise to destroy the Treaty of Versailles. They don't show the appeal to racist people who hated the Jews. No there is not enough information in these two sources alone.

Examiner's Comments on: Answer 1

This is an answer with too many generalities. For example, the first sentence is a rote answer, that is, an answer that has been learnt by heart and is not linked to the specific question. The second sentence is slightly silly and no reason is given for the figures being made up. If you are told that these are figures of election results and unemployment, then that is what they are. If it was about Hitler saying how many people write thanking him for being a good leader, that might be different. The question only starts to get answered in the third sentence, where the student begins to use some of his/her own knowledge. But there is no mention of things that the statistics do not show. This answer would get 2–3 marks.

Answer 2

This has the beginnings of a good answer. It states what the sources do tell us, and then it explains what is missing. It shows background knowledge, however it is thin on detail and the candidate does not suggest other sources that could be used to achieve the required information. Nor does the answer consider how Nazi support went down in November 1932, although unemployment continued to rise. This would get 4 marks.

Now it is your turn. Answer the question. Then compare your answer with the two given above.

8. The Nazis take Power

1. Topic Summary

Between January 1933 and August 1934, Hitler set about establishing a dictatorship. He knew he had to achieve this by legal means after his experience following the Munich Putsch. Hitler wanted to establish his complete control over government, and other political parties.

2. What do I Need to Know?

How Hitler gained total power, what were the steps he took and why no one seemed able to stop him. You need to understand the importance of events such as the Reichstag fire, the Enabling Law and the Night of the Long Knives.

3. History of Hitler's rise to Dictatorship

Hitler becomes Chancellor

By 1932 the Depression was biting hard in Germany and support for the Nazis grew. In the July 1932 elections to the Reichstag they won 230 seats and although this fell back to 196 in the November election, they were still the largest party.

- In January 1933 Hitler was appointed Chancellor but with only three other Nazis in the government itself. Ex-Chancellor Papen was appointed Hitler's deputy to help 'control' him.
- Hitler immediately called another general election, hoping to win a majority of seats. He hoped to use his position as Chancellor to win more support for the Nazi Party.
- In February 1933 the Reichstag was set alight and a communist called Van Der Lubbe was caught inside the building.
- The fire gave Hitler the excuse to pass emergency laws to 'protect' the country without having to get the support of the Reichstag.
- Hitler banned the Communist Party from campaigning in the election and he limited the activities of the other parties.
- Some felt that the 'luck' of the fire was too much of a coincidence. They believed the fire was started by the Nazis themselves. However, evidence does not seem to back this up.

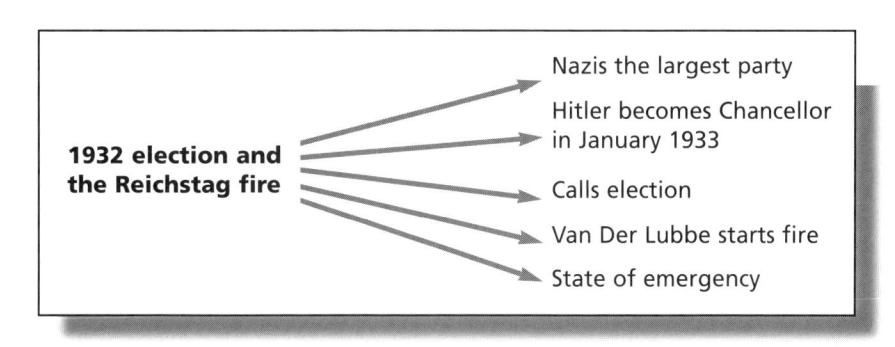

Summary box 1

1932 election and the Reichstag fire
- Nazis the largest party
- Hitler becomes Chancellor in January 1933
- Calls election
- Van Der Lubbe starts fire
- State of emergency

1933 election and the Enabling Law

- In the 1933 election the Nazis won 44 per cent of the vote — 288 seats — but failed to win a majority of seats.
- Hitler wanted to change the Constitution. To do this he actually needed 66 per cent of the seats. Even when the Nazis and Nationalists joined together, Hitler could not achieve this.
- He then used the Reichstag fire and Van Der Lubbe's conviction to ban the Communist Party and prevent the 81 Communist deputies from taking up their seats.
- Then Hitler used his SA to bully and cajole members of the Reichstag to vote for the Enabling Law. This was passed by 444 votes to 94. Only the Social Democrats voted against Hitler.
- The Enabling Law granted Hitler the right to make laws without consulting the Reichstag for a period of four years.
- One of Hitler's first actions was to ban all other political parties. Only the Nazi Party had a legal right to exist. Hitler had established himself as dictator in Germany — and had done so by using legal means.

Summary box 2

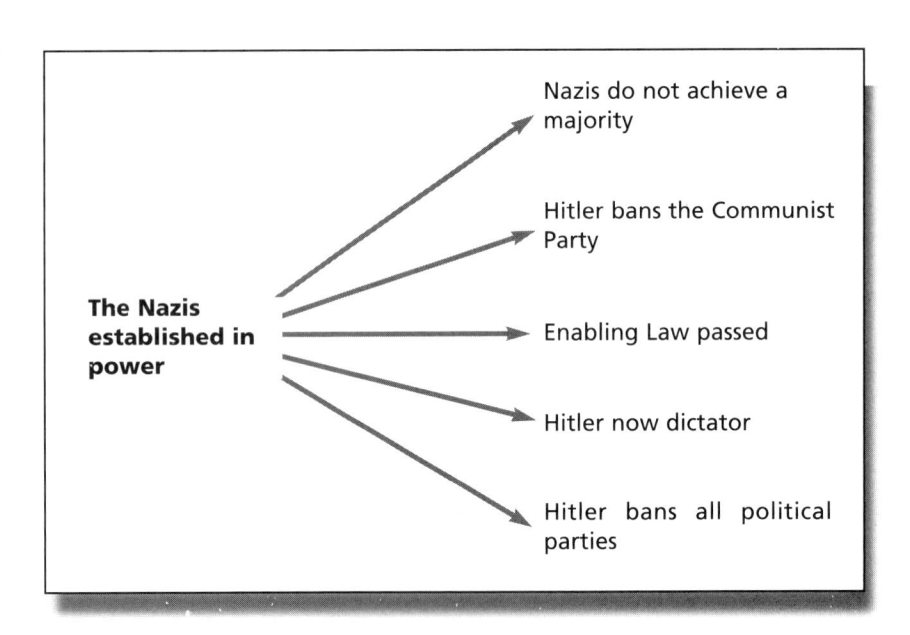

The Nazis established in power
- Nazis do not achieve a majority
- Hitler bans the Communist Party
- Enabling Law passed
- Hitler now dictator
- Hitler bans all political parties

Winning the support of the army

- Hitler realised that to maintain himself in power he needed the support of the army. He had this because the army approved of Hitler's plans to rearm and overturn the Treaty of Versailles.
- But army officers did not like the SA, Hitler's private bodyguard. The leader of the SA, Ernst Rohm, openly criticised the army for being full of 'old fogeys'. He wanted the SA to replace them.

- Hitler could not afford to lose army support so on the 30 June 1934 he ordered the murder of the leadership of the SA, along with many of his political rivals. Most important was Rohm's murder.

Hitler becomes Fuhrer
- On 2 August 1934, Hindenburg died. Hitler made himself President, though he adopted the title 'Fuhrer'.
- Every soldier had to pledge an oath of personal loyalty to Hitler, not the country.

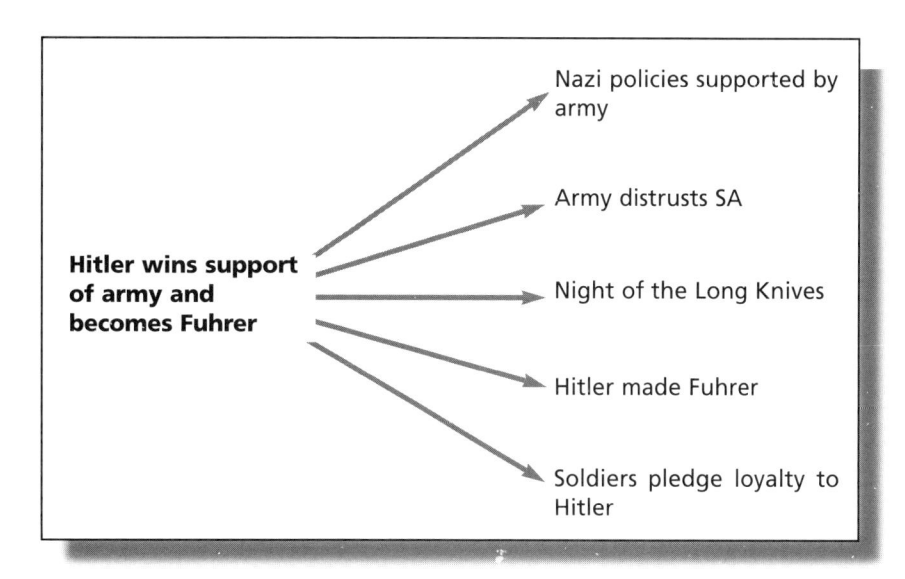

Summary box 3

Hitler wins support of army and becomes Fuhrer
- Nazi policies supported by army
- Army distrusts SA
- Night of the Long Knives
- Hitler made Fuhrer
- Soldiers pledge loyalty to Hitler

Task Copy out this table and fill the gaps to give a summary of Hitler's actions in power during 1933 and 1934.

Date	Event	Consequences
January 1933	Hitler becomes Chancellor	
February 1933		Hitler able to call a state of emergency
1933		Nazis win 44% of votes
March 1933	Enabling Law passed	
July 1933		No opposition in the Reichstag
	Night of the Long Knives	
August 1934		Hitler combines Chancellor, President and commander-in chief of the army. Hitler is Fuhrer.
August	Oath of Allegiance	

The Nazis take Power

4 What do I Know?

Once you have revised this topic thoroughly you should be able to answer most of these questions without using your notes. How many can you get right?

1. Why was Hitler not in complete control when he was made Chancellor in January 1933?
2. When was the Reichstag fire?
3. Why was the fire a 'stroke of luck' for the Nazis?
4. What was the percentage of Nazi votes in the 1933 election?
5. What percentage had Hitler hoped to gain?
6. Which party was Hitler's ally in the Reichstag?
7. Who did Hitler ban straight after the election?
8. What law was passed by a majority of 444 votes to 94 in March 1933?
9. What did Hitler do to the other political parties just after the passing of this law?
10. Who called the army a bunch of 'old fogeys'?
11. What happened on the 30 June 1934?
12. Who died on 2 August 1934?
13. What new title did Hitler adopt in 1934?
14. What change was made to the army's oath of loyalty?
15. What do we mean when we call Hitler's government 'totalitarian'?

My score ....

What is important about:
- The Reichstag fire
- The Enabling Law
- The Night of the Long The Knives
- The Oath of Allegiance?

5 Key Dates to Learn

1933	30 January	Hitler becomes Chancellor
	27 February	Reichstag fire
	23 March	Enabling Act
	14 July	All political parties banned except Nazis
	19 October	Germany leaves the League of Nations
1934	30 June	Night of the Long Knives
	2 August	Hitler becomes President.

The Nazis take Power

6. Using the Sources

Cartoons are a very useful way of getting a lot of information into one small source. Look closely at the Sources A and B and read the notes that follows.

Source A

▲ A British cartoon showing Hitler dressed up as the Kaiser.

Source B

▲ A British cartoon showing Hitler to be no more than another Nero — the Roman emperor who supposedly burned down Rome.

The Nazis take Power

What can we learn from these sources? If we look at Source A we can see that the artist is trying to state that Hitler wants to be just like the Kaiser before the First World War. Hitler is shown as a child who has found a game: dressing up. The clothes are too big for Hitler, they make him look foolish. Hitler's parents, meaning the German people, obviously don't take his actions seriously. On the floor are some of Hitler's ideas. They are called 'bunk' and 'trash', meaning rubbish.

It is also important to note that this is a British cartoon. It will be from a British point of view. It will also be seeing the events based on how the British regarded Hitler. The German people saw him in a very different light. To many he was a hero who would lead them out of the humiliation of the Treaty of Versailles.

Source B concerns the specific events of the Reichstag fire. The cartoonist compares this event with that of when Emperor Nero burned down Rome so that he could have complete control. The man behind Hitler is Hindenburg. The cartoonist suggests that he is encouraging Hitler to use the event to become dictator, using his emergency powers. The people accused of starting the fire are the Communists, as indicated in the caption where they are called 'the Red Peril'.

Exam Type Questions

> Examine the cartoon below. How useful is this source to an historian studying the Night of the Long Knives? Explain your answer as fully as possible. **(7 marks)**

THEY SALUTE WITH BOTH HANDS NOW.

▲ A British cartoon showing the SA surrendering to Hitler.

The Nazis take Power

Answer 1

This source is very useful to an historian because it gives us a lot of information which I know is true. Hitler did order the murder of the leaders of the SA, and these are the dead bodies. Hitler did this in order to win the support of the army, who are shown around the outside. The action gave him control of the SA, as shown by the raised hands. The word 'double-cross' on his arm shows that he has double-crossed his former friends.

Answer 2

The source is very useful to an historian because the information it contains seems to agree with my own background knowledge. For example, Hitler did order the executions of many important people. We can see the dead bodies. The army was involved but not directly. They did not kill anyone, but if Hitler had not been trying to please the army, the Night of the Long Knives would not have taken place. The army is shown a distance away from the killing.

However, there are many things the source does not tell us. For example, it does not mention that Rohm was a political rival of Hitler. Also the cartoon was drawn from a British point of view. People in Britain were shocked by the event and so the cartoon would reflect their feelings. To get a balanced viewpoint we would need some comment from a German source, maybe a diary hidden from the Gestapo, so that it was not censored by the Nazis.

Examiner's Comments on: Answer 1

The candidate has tried to explain what it is that the cartoon tells us, but does not indicate what is missing, e.g. the personal rivalry with Rohm. Nor does the answer address the nature of the source itself. Are there any problems with using a British cartoon to look at Hitler's actions? The answer would get 3 marks.

Answer 2

I like this answer as it does try to explain what is good about the source, but at the same time it does hint at what problems the source presents. I would have liked to have seen greater detail on these points, but the answer gives enough information to show that the candidate understands the point being made. This would get 6 marks.

Practice Question

Now answer the question yourself. Work out the meaning of the different parts of the cartoon. Think about the smoking gun; the army in the background; the papers on the floor; the dead bodies; and Hitler's arm band. Then compare your answer with the two given above.

9. Hitler in Power

1. Topic Summary

The period 1934 to 1945 was a time of totalitarian dictatorship in Germany. All power rested, at least in name, with Hitler. To make sure that the vast majority of citizens went along with his orders a series of measures were introduced. Some of these were meant to frightened the people into submission; but some brought positive improvements in the lives of ordinary Germans. Some historians say that Hitler used the 'carrot and stick' approach. He gave people what they wanted ('the carrot'), but also used force ('the stick'). Opponents of Hitler only became bold enough to try to overthrow him when news of defeats in the war reached the German people.

2. What do I Need to Know?

You will need to know the methods by which Hitler controlled the people. You will also need to know the policies he employed to bring economic success back to Germany. You must not see this time as simply one of oppression. Nor must you dwell on the treatment of the Jews. Whilst this is important, it must be remembered that this is just one element of Nazi Germany.

3. The History of Nazi Germany

Totalitarian dictatorship

- All opposition to the Nazi Party was banned. To voice dissent or suggest alternatives was to commit treason, punishable by imprisonment in a concentration camp. Hitler wanted all sections of society under his control.
- Hitler abolished the federal system of government. Individual states did not exist after 30 January 1934.
- Hitler 'Nazified' the civil service to make sure it followed his policies. He made sure there were no public demonstrations against him and removed any opponents of his regime, such as Jews, from the civil service.
- Hitler controlled all this by making sure that all power began with himself. The Party controlled Germany; Hitler controlled the Party.

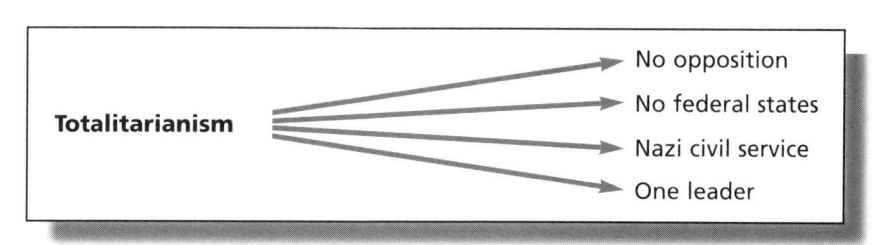

Summary box 1

Totalitarianism
- No opposition
- No federal states
- Nazi civil service
- One leader

Law and order: SS and the Gestapo

- Hitler was not interested in justice, he was interested in social order and control.
- Hitler made the law, but he wanted to control the judges. Unreliable judges, such as Jews and liberals, were removed. Those that remained were put under strict control.
- Judges were expected to reflect the desires of the Nazi Party, not those of justice. Hitler often interfered if he felt sentences were too lenient.
- A lot of 'justice' did not get as far as the courts. Hitler used the SS to strike terror into most Germans. The SS was ruthless, and utterly dedicated to Hitler.
- The Gestapo (secret police) arrested people for criticising the Nazis. Ordinary criminals were treated better than political ones. There were no restraints on the Gestapo in its task to protect the Nazi regime.
- People were encouraged to report on anti-Nazi activity by their neighbours, work mates, friends, even their own family. Anyone accused was rarely released. Most were sent straight to the concentration camps, without getting a trial.

Summary box 2

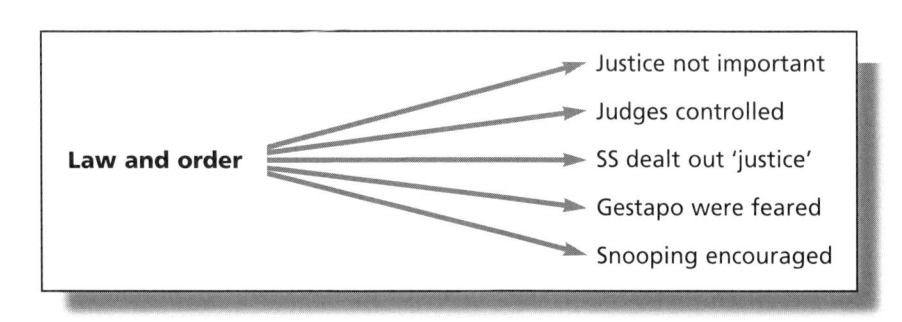

Law and order:
- Justice not important
- Judges controlled
- SS dealt out 'justice'
- Gestapo were feared
- Snooping encouraged

Propaganda and education

Control of media

- Josef Goebbels was the Minister of Propaganda and Enlightenment. It was one of the most important jobs in Nazi Germany. He controlled what Germans heard and read and what children were taught.
- All films, books, records, newspapers, radio broadcasts and posters were controlled. Nothing could be written, drawn or said without the approval of Goebbels.
- Cheap radios were provided in order that all citizens could hear Hitler's speeches. Factories, shops and schools were expected to stop work in order to hear them. In this way the German people were fed a continual message praising the Nazis and criticising their opponents.
- Goebbels made sure that groups, such as the Jews, were seen in a negative way and that Hitler was seen as a god-like figure.

Educating the Nazi way

- The Nazis completely controlled the schools to make sure the children were taught the Nazi way of seeing things.
- All teachers had to be Nazis. All lessons had to reflect Nazi ideology. Children were taught to see Jews as parasites.
- Every child was taught to be fit and ready to fight for the Fatherland. Greater emphasis was placed on physical education rather than academic learning.
- Girls were taught to be good mothers and wives.
- Hitler Youth was set up to control how the young spent their leisure time. It aimed to indoctrinate the young with Nazi ideas and help make them physically strong, either for the army or for the Motherland.

Summary box 3

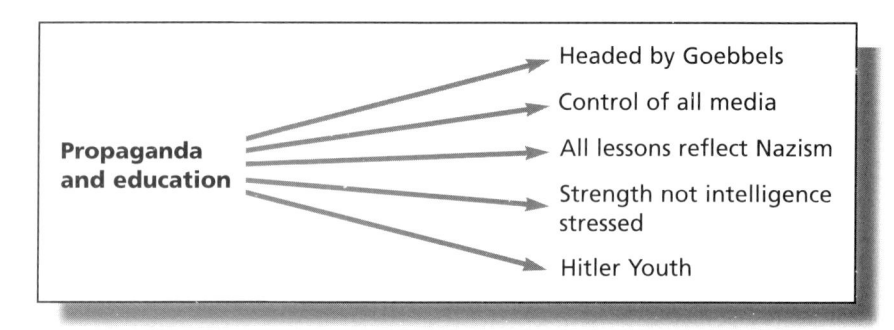

Propaganda and education
- Headed by Goebbels
- Control of all media
- All lessons reflect Nazism
- Strength not intelligence stressed
- Hitler Youth

Treatment of the Jews

- Almost immediately any Jews who were civil servants, teachers, or employed in any other government jobs, were sacked.
- The SA were posted outside Jewish shops to persuade people not to shop in them.
- In 1935, Jews were banned from parks, swimming pools, restaurants and public buildings.
- The Nuremberg Laws took away their rights as citizens. And they could not be married to Germans, even if they were already married!
- In 1938 thousands of Jewish shops and synagogues were destroyed in the Kristallnacht. Over 40,000 Jews were sent to concentration camps.
- After 1941, the 'Final Solution' of the Jewish problem was started, with the systematic killing of millions of Jews in extermination camps, such as Auschwitz, Treblinka and Sobibor.

Summary box 4

Treatment of the Jews
- Banned from government posts
- Jewish shops boycotted
- Banned from public places
- Nuremberg Laws
- Kristallnacht
- Final Solution

The Nazi economy

In 1933 there were 6 million unemployed in Germany, by 1938 there were less than half a million. Hitler had solved the problem of unemployment in several ways.

- He created jobs by spending millions of marks on public works, such as house and road building, and by increasing the armed forces. Men became soldiers and jobs were created in those industries which supplied the armed forces: weapons, uniforms, food etc.
- He forced many people, such as Jews and women, out of work, to be replaced by German men.
- He banned trade unions. This meant that wages could fall, so more workers were used.
- While the economy never reached the levels of the Stresemann era, many Germans remembered the Depression and were grateful for Hitler's actions.

Hitler's plan was to make Germany self-sufficient. This is called autarchy.

Summary box 5

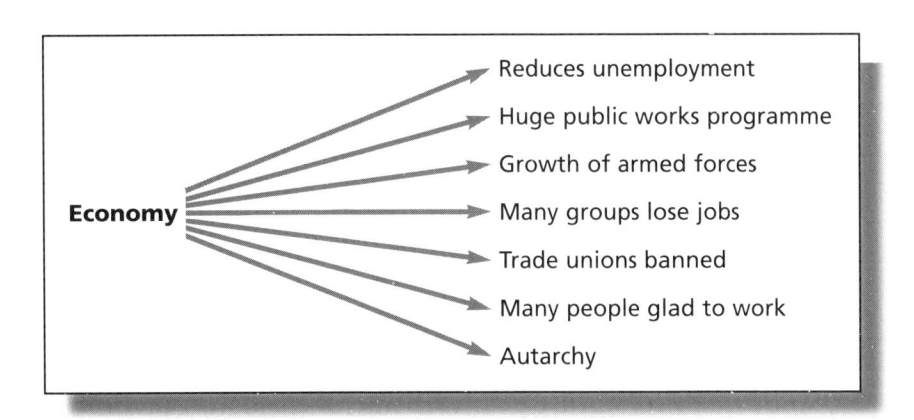

Economy →
- Reduces unemployment
- Huge public works programme
- Growth of armed forces
- Many groups lose jobs
- Trade unions banned
- Many people glad to work
- Autarchy

Work and leisure

Hitler had banned trade unions, but he did try to cover their work with three organisations.

- The German Labour Front, which regulated wages and hours of work. Usually the pay went down and the hours became longer.
- The Beauty of Labour, which controlled conditions at work, the idea being that if you were happy at work, you would willingly work longer hours.
- Strength Through Joy, which provided leisure activities. Good workers were rewarded with a range of leisure activities, such as football, winter sports and even cruises.

Workers were persuaded through propaganda that they were helping the Fatherland and that their lives were better than those of fellow workers in Russia or the West.

Summary box 6

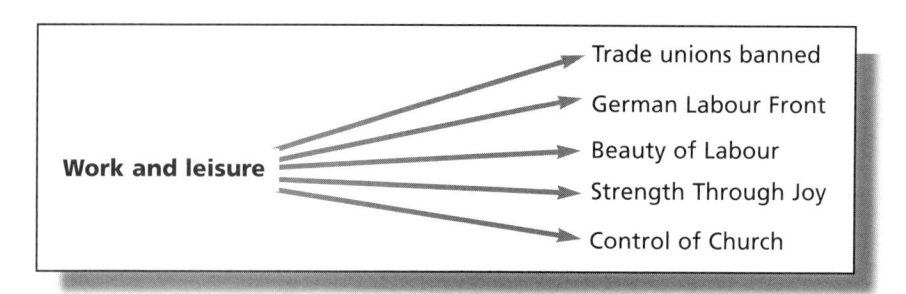

Work and leisure
- Trade unions banned
- German Labour Front
- Beauty of Labour
- Strength Through Joy
- Control of Church

Church

- Hitler opposed the Church as a group beyond his control.
- Hitler signed a concordat with the Catholic Church in 1933. He agreed not to interfere in Church matters if the Church kept out of politics.
- Hitler united all the Protestant Churches into one Reich Church.
- Protestants who opposed this, such as Pastor Niemuller, were sent to concentration camps.

Life for civilians during the war

- The period 1939–41 saw a rise in the standard of living for many Germans. Although most foodstuffs were rationed, 40 per cent of Germans ate better than before the war.
- Many goods were brought back from conquered countries.

But:

- The invasion of Russia in 1941 led to more families losing loved ones or having their men wounded.
- Propaganda reassured the German people that despite setbacks the war could still be won.
- By 1943 it was impossible to conceal that the war was going badly. Rations were severely cut back and non-essential shops and businesses were closed down.
- The people were suffering heavy bombardment by the Allies. The irony was that the air raids united Nazi and anti-Nazi against the Allies.
- By 1944 it was obvious that the war was lost. Thousands of refugees were pouring into Germany.
- The government lost control. Ration cards were ignored and sometimes food could only be bought through the black market.
- Hitler committed suicide in April 1945.

Summary box 7

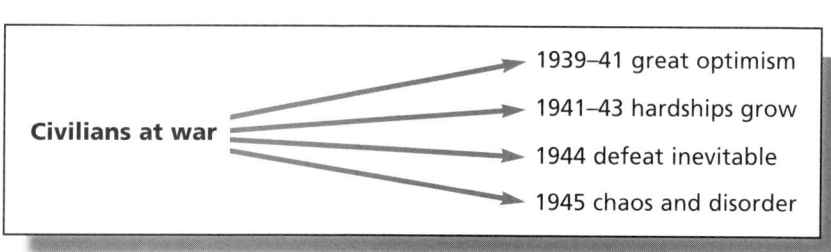

Civilians at war
- 1939–41 great optimism
- 1941–43 hardships grow
- 1944 defeat inevitable
- 1945 chaos and disorder

Hitler in Power

4 What do I Know?

Once you have revised this topic thoroughly you should be able to answer most of these questions without using your notes. How many can you get right?

1. Why could Hitler be said to have used a 'carrot and stick' approach?
2. What name was given to the German secret police?
3. Where were political prisoners sent?
4. What was the purpose of the Minister of Propaganda and Enlightenment?
5. In which year was the Olympic Games held in Berlin?
6. Why do you think Hitler was so keen to control education?
7. What were the Laws that limited the rights of Jews in 1935?
8. What was the Kristallnacht?
9. How many unemployed were there in 1933?
10. How was unemployment brought down by 1938?
11. What is autarchy?
12. Which organisation improved working conditions?
13. Which organisation organised leisure activities?
14. What was the Holocaust?
15. When did Hitler die?

My score ....

What was important about:
- The Gestapo
- Propaganda
- Autarchy
- The Hitler Youth
- The concordat?

5 Key Dates to Learn

1933		Trade unions banned
1934	2 August	Hitler becomes Fuhrer
1935	9 September	Nuremberg 'Race' Laws
1936		Olympic Games
1938	8 November	Kristallnacht
1939		Germany invades Poland. Second World War begins
1941		Final Solution begins Invasion of Russia
1945		Hitler commits suicide. Second World War ends.

73

Hitler in Power

6 Using the Source

Look at the source below and answer the question that follows.

▲ Poster showing the importance of radio.

> What does the poster in the source tell us about Nazi propaganda?

Hints for answer

The source shows a radio. The radio was very important for Nazi propaganda. Goebbels, the Nazi Minister for Propaganda, wanted to ensure that *all* Germans could hear Hitler's speeches. So radios were sold cheaply to the people, and every school and factory had to broadcast Nazi speeches. The poster gives a sense of 'belonging', of being part of the German nation

74

7. Exam Type Questions

This kind of exam question requires candidates to write an essay. Look at the answer to the question and at the examiner's comments. Then read the notes that follow before answering the question yourself.

> How did Hitler control the German people between 1933 and 1939? How successful was he in maintaining his control?
>
> **(15 marks)**

Answer

Hitler kept control in Germany by not only giving the people what they wanted, but also making sure that he had total control over them. He was to be very successful in maintaining his control.

From the start, Hitler used the SS and the Gestapo to keep a close check on any opposition to his rule. Anybody who showed their opposition to Hitler was quickly sent to the concentration camps. Dachau was opened in 1933. It was full of Communists and Social Democrats. People were encouraged to 'tell' on their friends and colleagues if they said anything against the state. Soon the word got around that you should keep your mouth shut if you did not want to end up in serious trouble.

Hitler's other main weapon in his control of the people was propaganda. Josef Goebbels controlled all forms of visual, written and spoken material seen by the German people. Everything had to reflect Nazi ideas. For example, jazz music was banned as it was 'black' music and blacks were considered inferior. Goebbels organised mass rallies and he also ensured that virtually every German had access to a radio to hear Hitler's speeches.

Hitler banned all opposition, both political parties and trade unions. Workers were expected to work longer hours for less pay, all for the good of the Fatherland. This however was only half the story. At work, Hitler also set about improving conditions through Beauty of Labour. He also tried to reward good workers with cheap sports and even luxury cruises. German workers were generally happy workers.

The other main point is that Hitler did solve unemployment as he had promised. Unemployment dropped from 6 million to less than 500,000. To most Germans this was the main concern. If they could provide for their families then they were much happier. It was not important enough to complain about the treatment of a few groups of people like the Jews that did not seem to agree with Hitler. Complaining would only result in being put in a concentration camp.

> As time went on, many Germans were impressed with Hitler's actions against Britain and France. Hitler seemed to be standing up to them, and making Germany a proud and strong nation again. Many people were not dedicated Nazis, but Hitler seemed to be doing a good job. It would not be until the setbacks in the Second World War that any serious attempt was made to overthrow him. I would say he was very successful in maintaining his control over the German people.

Examiner's Comments

I like this answer. It starts by answering the question and then looks at the negative and positive aspects of control. It also sticks to what is relevant (e.g. no mention of the Holocaust because that was after 1939).

The answer tries to give examples to back up the points made. But it needs to expand the points in more detail. For example, there is only a brief mention of the treatment of Jews, and reference to the Nuremberg Laws or Kristallnacht would have been good. The candidate knows the answer to the question and would score something around 12 marks. If more knowledge had been used to support the answer this would have got very high marks.

Practice Question

An essay can be the hardest part of an exam. It requires a long answer with lots of facts and points, yet you are expected to know all the information as no sources are given to help you. How do you go about answering the essay?

1. Revise. This gives you the information in order to have any chance of answering the question.

2. Answer the question set. This may seem obvious, but too many students start writing pages on the Holocaust when the question is on Nazi education! The student writes about the mass killings, the concentration camps etc, when they needed to be discussing school timetables and the curriculum. You must make sure you produce only relevant material.

    It is a good idea to begin your essay by answering the question and then using the rest of the essay to support what you say.

3. If you make a statement, you must have a fact to back it up. For example, you might say that Hitler was ruthless and would do anything to gain power. This is your statement. A fact to back it up would be the Night of the Long Knives, where Hitler ordered the murder of some of his closest friends and followers.

4. Answer as fully as you can. Do not try to answer the question in five lines. You can't! If the question is worth 15 marks then write at least a page and a half, if not two!

5 Give both sides to any point you make (if there are two sides of course). If the essay is about unemployment, you should mention that Hitler reduced unemployment from six million to three million in one year, through rearmament and building works. However, he was also able to reduce unemployment by sacking Jewish, communist and women workers and giving their jobs to unemployed German men.

Now answer the above question yourself. Then compare your answer with the one given.

The USA, 1919–45

10. Isolation, 1919–24

1. Topic Summary

By the end of the First World War world politics was changing. The United States did well out of the war but many Americans resented involvement in events 'over there'. During the next 20 years America avoided getting involved in disputes and wars between other countries. It concentrated on increasing its wealth and trying to make sure its people enjoyed life to the full. Even as early as 1928 the President of the time proclaimed the 'end of poverty', though this was not true for many people.

2. What do I Need to Know?

You will need to know the reasons why America wished to turn its back on the rest of the world. You will also need to understand how this helped create an economic boom.

3. History of American Isolationism

First World War, the Treaty of Versailles and isolationism

- In 1917, America joined the First World War on the side of Britain and France. Germany was shown to be the aggressor.
- After the war President Wilson put forward his Fourteen Points to help create a better world. Britain and France did not support Wilson. Both seemed set on revenge and their own interests.
- Americans who believed they had been fighting for freedom now believed they had just been tricked into helping Britain and France. The American people felt cheated.
- Many Americans were immigrants from Europe, but had left to get away from the old squabbles and disputes. Now they found they had been drawn back into them.
- Many American politicians understood this and stood for election as isolationists. In the 1920 elections they were elected.
- Isolationism meant that America would not join the League of Nations, just when the world needed it. President Woodrow Wilson tried to persuade his country to join, without success.

Summary box 1

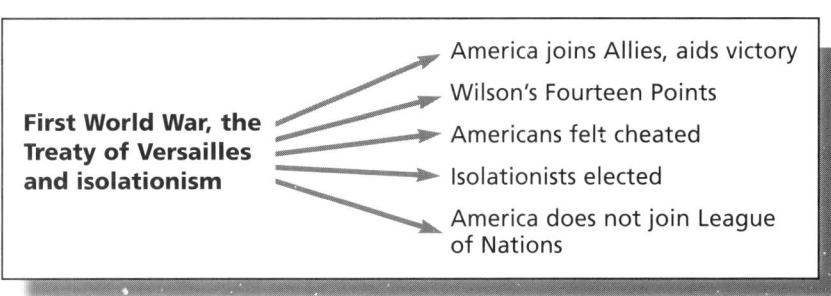

First World War, the Treaty of Versailles and isolationism
- America joins Allies, aids victory
- Wilson's Fourteen Points
- Americans felt cheated
- Isolationists elected
- America does not join League of Nations

Immigration quotas

- America was seen as a country that welcomed immigrants. Many of its people had come from other countries to settle there. It was the land of opportunity — a place to make your fortune; you could start off poor and still become very rich.
- Most immigrants had come from Europe and settled in well. America needed more new people to farm the new lands and more workers for the new industries.

But:

- After the First World War the American public was worried that the 'wrong sort' of immigrant was coming into their country.
- They were not White Anglo-Saxon Protestants (WASPs). They were Catholics from Italy, or Jews from Russia. And those immigrants already there felt threatened by the new arrivals.
- There were various reasons why Americans wanted to limit the number of immigrants:
    - Immigrants from Russia were believed to be communists.
    - Some immigrants did not bother to learn to speak English.
    - Many immigrants were willing to work for lower pay than Americans.
    - Some immigrants did not pledge allegiance to the American flag.
- 1921 Immigration Quota Act passed. The quota was 3 per cent of the 1910 population. This limited the number of immigrants.
- 1924 National Origins Act passed. The quota changed to 2 per cent of the 1890 population. This ensured more immigrants from Britain and Germany and less from Italy and Russia.

Summary box 2

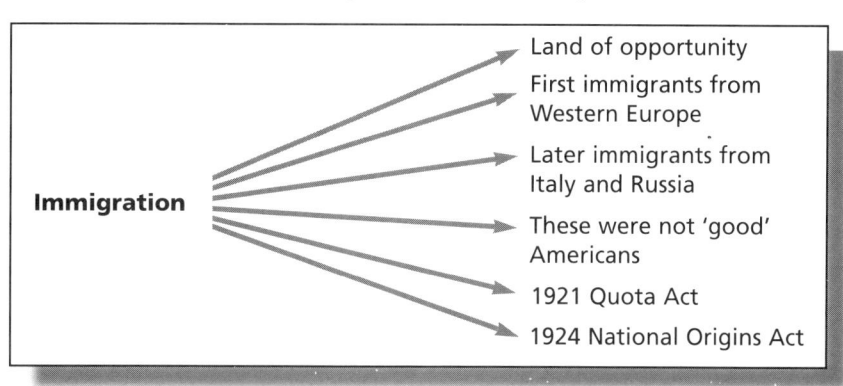

Immigration
- Land of opportunity
- First immigrants from Western Europe
- Later immigrants from Italy and Russia
- These were not 'good' Americans
- 1921 Quota Act
- 1924 National Origins Act

Tariff controls: 'economic isolationism'

- American business knew that after the First World War, British, French and German companies would try to sell their goods to the American public.
- American business also knew that they would not be able to sell many goods in Europe where the long war had left many people poor.
- To make sure the American people bought their goods from American businesses, the American government set high tariffs (taxes) on all foreign goods entering America.
- The government passed the Fordney-McCumber Tariff Act in 1922. In 1929 they passed the Hawley Smoot Tariff Act.

Isolation, 1919–24

- Tarrifs made American goods cheaper than foreign goods. So Americans would buy American goods. This policy is called protectionism. American companies were able to make huge profits because of it. And they employed lots of workers who earned high wages compared to people in Europe.
- Foreign countries tried to retaliate by putting high tariffs on American goods entering their countries. Most American companies did not care because they could never produce enough to sell in America alone. They did not need to sell their goods abroad.
- But some businesses were badly hit. For example, the farmers and the older industries, such as textiles and coal mining, needed to sell their goods abroad.

However, the American government was more interested in helping the new industries, such as the makers of cars and electrical goods. Farmers and the older industries suffered badly.

Summary box 3

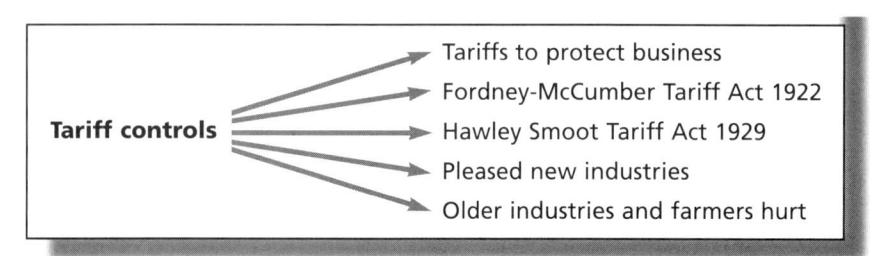

Tariff controls
- Tariffs to protect business
- Fordney-McCumber Tariff Act 1922
- Hawley Smoot Tariff Act 1929
- Pleased new industries
- Older industries and farmers hurt

4 What do I Know?

Once you have revised this topic thoroughly you should be able to answer most of these questions without using your notes. How many can you get right?

1. In which year did America join the First World War?
2. What were the Fourteen Points?
3. Who was America's president in 1918?
4. What is isolationism?
5. Why did America adopt this policy?
6. Where had most of America's early immigrants come from?
7. What does WASP stand for?
8. What objections did people have to the 'new immigrants' after the First World War?
9. What was the quota system for immigrants in 1921?
10. What was the quota system in 1924?
11. What year was the Fordney-McCumber Tariff Act passed?
12. What is the name of the system that protects industry from foreign competition?
13. Which types of industries supported these tariffs?
14. Which types of industries were opposed to these tariffs?
15. Is it true that all the American people prospered after the war?

My score ....

What is important about:
- Isolationism
- Immigration quotas
- Tariff controls?

Isolation, 1919–24

5. Key Dates to Learn

- **1917** America enters First World War
- **1918** First World War ends
- **1922** Fordney-McCumber Tariff Act
- **1924** Immigration Act.

6. Using the Sources

Look at Sources A and B and answer the questions.

Source A

'The question is whether we can refuse the moral leadership that is offered us, whether we shall accept or reject the confidence of the world.'

▲ From a speech by Woodrow Wilson, 1919.

Source B

'Wilson has no authority whatsoever to speak for the American people at this time ... His Fourteen Points and all his utterances every which way have ceased to have any shadow of right to be accepted as expressive of the will of the American people.'

▲ From a speech by Theodore Roosevelt, 1919.

1. What did Wilson mean by his comment in Source A?
2. What were the Fourteen Points mentioned in Source B?
3. How might Wilson reject the statement that he has no right to 'speak for the American people'?
4. How was Roosevelt proved right in his comment that Wilson was not following 'the will of the American people'?

7. Exam Type Question

Sometimes exam boards use statistics in questions. Let's have a look at how we can answer this sort of question.

How useful are the following sources to an historian studying the topic of immigration into America in the first part of the century? Explain your answer fully. **(7 marks)**

Isolation, 1919–24

Source A

Country of immigrant's origin	1921 3 % of 1910 population	1924 2 % of 1890 population
Germany	68,059	51,227
British Isles, including Ireland	77,342	62,574
Sweden and Norway	32,244	16,014
Poland	25,827	5,982
Italy	42,957	3,845
Czechoslovakia	14,382	3,073
Russia	34,284	2,248
All countries	356,995	164,667

▲ The effects of the quota system introduced in 1924. This shows the maximum number of immigrants allowed from each country each year.

Source B

	1881–90	1901–10	1931–40
Germany	1,453,000	341,000	114,000
British Isles	1,462,000	865,000	42,000
Scandinavia	656,000	505,000	11,000
Italy	307,000	2,046,000	68,000
Russia	213,000	1,597,000	1,000
Asia	70,000	324,000	16,000
Others	1,086,000	3,117,000	276,000
Total	5,247,000	8,795,000	528,000

▲ The number of immigrants actually entering the United States from other countries.

Answer 1

I think that Sources A and B might not be any use to an historian because they are statistics, and statistics can lie. How do we know that these are correct? The two sources do tell us about the numbers allowed into the country and show that the numbers had fallen between 1900 and 1930. I would need to have a lot more information to fully answer this question.

Answer 2

I think that an historian would find Source A and Source B of some use, but not completely. From Source A you can work out how many people were allowed into America and how that would have altered the make-up of the different nationalities (as a percentage) within the country. We can see that the British and German populations rose but not the Italian or Russian. Source B is very good for the

Isolation, 1919–24

> exact numbers of immigrants entering America. We know that more came from Italy than from anywhere else. We can see the actual results of the 1924 Immigration Act.
>
> However, neither source really gives us the reasons why the number of immigrants were limited. They do not give the numbers of Communist Party members or the numbers who could not speak English, either when they arrived or after they had settled in. To know the reasons for the 1924 Immigration Act, and its social consequences, we would need more evidence. Data of the educational standards of the newer immigrants and the growth in political parties, such as the Communists, might be shown in election results, etc.

Examiner's Comments on: Answer 1

I am not certain what the candidate hopes to achieve with this answer. The biggest problem with candidates in an exam is that they often use generalisations, such as 'statistics can lie' or 'the camera never lies', which are quite simply mistaken. Although we are not told where the figures come from, we have no reason whatsoever to think that they are not true. The answer also fails to fully analyse the sources. What do they tell us? Is it valuable information? The last statement also adds little. You need to give specific points. So what information do you need? This answer only deserves 1 mark for saying that the sources show that the numbers have fallen.

Answer 2

This answer tries to look at the different approaches needed for this question. It explains what the sources do tell us. It then explains what is missing and how to possibly find this information. While the arguments are not fully developed in places, for example the suggested list of different sources is a little weak, it tries to be specific and gives a reason for the points. I would give it 6 marks.

Practice Question

Now answer the question yourself. Then compare your answer with the above answers. Remember that to answer a question on usefulness you need to look at the following points:

1 What information do(es) the source(s) contain? Is it relevant to the question set?
2 What information is missing from the source(s)? Is this missing information vital, or can the historian get most of what they need from the source(s) provided?
3 You might need to assess the reliability of the source. However *do not* make the mistake of suggesting a source is of no use because it is unreliable. Think what it could therefore be reliable for.

Sources A and B contain a great deal of useful information for an historian. It is sometimes difficult to be able to extract this information though. Below is an example of what sort of things you might learn from the two sources.

- Source A tells us that the American government halved (356,995 to 164,667) the number of immigrants that could possibly enter the United States. This does not mean that these are the exact numbers coming in. A quota is the maximum allowed.
- Source A also tells us that the largest sections of society in the United States were those of German or British origin. We can tell this from the fact that the quota allowed is based on numbers already in the country. (In 1924 given as 2% of the 1890 population.)
- Source A suggests that the quota rules were changed with the intention of lessening the numbers of immigrants from countries such as Italy and Russia, whilst at the same time maintaining the number of immigrants from Germany and the British Isles. While the number of Italian and Russian immigrants fell by over 90 per cent (the Russian quota fell from 34,284 in 1921 to 2,248 in 1924), the numbers of German and British immigrants only fell by about 20 per cent. (The British quota fell from 77,342 in 1921 to 62,574 in 1924, a drop of just under 15,000.) In this system the number of the 'right kind' of immigrants was assured to be higher than those from 'undesirable' countries.
- Source B shows the effect of the Immigration Act of 1924. The overall number of immigrants has fallen from 1881-90 to 1931-40, a fall of about 90 per cent (from 5,247,000 to 528,000). America was really cutting back on the number of immigrants.
- Source B also suggests that before the First World War, immigration was on the increase (from 5,247,000 to 8,795,000). However the countries of origin have changed. Whereas in 1881-90 most immigrants came from Germany and the British Isles (1,453,000 and 1,462,000 respectfully), by 1901-10 most immigrants came from Italy and Russia (2,046,000 and 1,597,000 respectfully). The 1924 Immigration Act seems to have reversed this trend. In the years 1931-40 the number of German immigrants is 114,000 compared to just 1,000 Russians.
- The problem with both the tables is that they do not show all the factors that affect immigration. (This is a problem with all statistics.) During the years 1931-40 Hitler came to power in Germany, and most of the German immigrants were Jews trying to escape Nazi persecution. Throughout the same period the Soviet government was making it almost impossible for anybody to leave their country. It is certain that more people wanted to leave Russia than actually could.

11. The 'Boom' Years: the USA in the 1920s

1. Topic Summary

For the American people the 1920s has been seen as a time of unlimited opportunities and wealth. America was the richest nation in history. In the 1920s the wages of many ordinary people rose, while the prices of goods either stayed the same or even fell. A wide range of consumer goods were produced to make people's lives easier. Many Americans expected to own a radio and a car.

This was called a 'boom' time, and for those sections of society who were part of this boom, life could not be better. However, for some sections of society — farmers, black people, workers in industries such as coal mining — it was not boom time. They wanted the good life, but they missed out because they just could not afford it.

2. What do I Need to Know?

You will be expected to know why it was that America became so rich in the 1920s. You will need to know the importance of industrialists such as Henry Ford. You will need to know how consumers were encouraged to spend their money. But you must also be aware that there was a darker side to America — in which people were not part of the boom; why organisations like the Ku Klux Klan were active; and why ordinary American citizens were willing to break the law and help the gangsters during Prohibition.

3. History of the 'Boom' Years

Boom time

- For the new industries, such as car production and electrical goods, this was a 'boom' time.
- Average wages rose from $1,158 a year in 1919 to $1,304 in 1927. The number of millionaires rose from 7,000 in 1914 to 35,000 in 1928.
- At the same time the prices of goods were actually falling; a Model T Ford cost $950 in 1913 but only $290 in 1927, so even more could be sold.
- As more and more people bought these new goods so the number of workers in the new industries grew.
- Advertising promised the American people all they could desire. Credit and hire-purchase schemes meant that more and more goods were bought.

- During the Presidential election of 1928, Hoover had claimed that there would soon be 'a chicken in every pot' and 'two cars in every garage'.
- It was not difficult to believe the idea that poverty was a thing of the past, that America would get richer and richer.

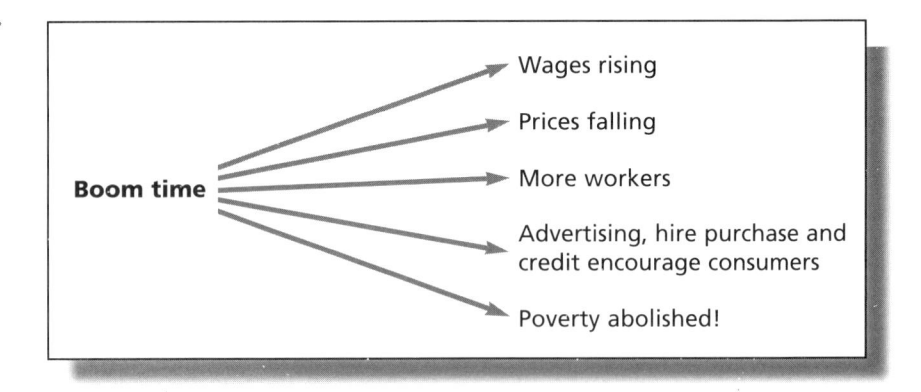

Summary box 1

Boom time →
- Wages rising
- Prices falling
- More workers
- Advertising, hire purchase and credit encourage consumers
- Poverty abolished!

Henry Ford and mass production

The industry that best summed up the boom time was car production. The car became a symbol of America.

- Henry Ford transformed the car industry. Ford made his cars on a production line. This is where each part of the car was assembled by one person, who then passed it down the line to the next person, who would assemble another part, and so on down the line until the car was complete.
- This increased the number of cars produced. In 1900 only 4,000 cars were made each year. By 1929 this had risen to 4.8 million a year. This is called mass production.
- Henry Ford used this system of a production line as an advertising slogan. He said, 'You can have any colour you like, as long as it is black.' He meant that all cars were made exactly the same.
- Not only did the car industry itself employ thousands of workers, it also created thousands of jobs in other industries:
  - steel for the body
  - glass for the windscreen
  - rubber for the tyres
  - car selling
  - road building
  - petrol stations
  - oil industry.
- For many people the car became a necessity rather than a luxury. They took it to work, on holiday and to the cinema or to the bars. Young men used it to take a girlfriend on a date, and so could avoid being watched by their parents.

Summary box 2

Henry Ford
- Car – a symbol of America
- Production line
- Mass production (Model T Ford)
- Boosts other industries

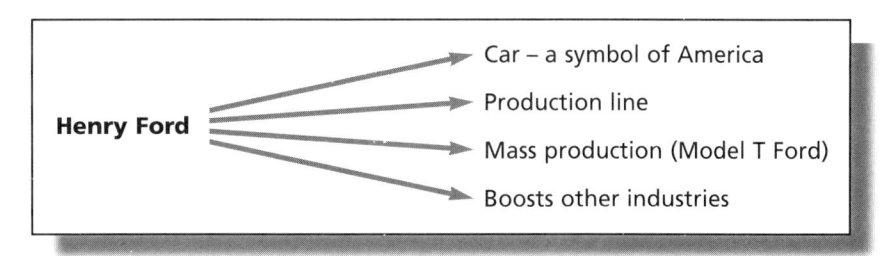

Entertainment

- A major effect of the boom was that Americans wanted to spend their disposable income on being entertained.
- People spent more on clothes, cigarettes and eating out. Virtually every house had a radio, even the homes of the poor. People loved to listen to jazz on the radio. They also heard adverts for the new consumer goods.
- People also loved going to the cinema. Hollywood was starting to control the film industry and was producing thousands of films each year.
- It was estimated that 100 million cinema tickets were sold each week. Actors, such as Charlie Chaplin and Greta Garbo, became celebrities.
- Night-clubs and listening to the jazz bands were also popular. People would drink, dance and have a good time. But drinking was illegal. The bars were run by gangsters and alcohol was banned.

Summary box 3

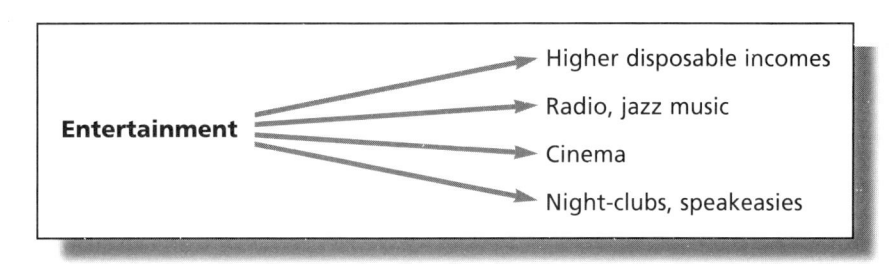

Entertainment
- Higher disposable incomes
- Radio, jazz music
- Cinema
- Night-clubs, speakeasies

Prohibition and gangsters
The fight against alcohol

- Temperance means not wanting to drink alcohol. Early in the century, temperance groups persuaded politicians to ban the sale of alcohol.
- Some of the arguments that they used were:
  - It was not Christian – most Americans believed in God
  - Alcohol was the cause of most fights in the streets
  - Workers would work harder without hangovers
  - Workers would miss fewer days due to illness
  - Children would not be left unattended at home or mistreated by a drunken parent
  - Fathers would spend the money on clothes and food, not waste it on drink.

- The Volstead Act (1919) was passed banning alcohol. This policy was called Prohibition. But soon home-made alcohol (moonshine) was being sold in illegal bars (speakeasies) in all the major towns and cities.
- Alcohol was also imported from other countries, such as Canada. This was called bootlegging.
- The main problem was that most Americans did not believe in temperance. They wanted to drink alcohol. Whoever could supply the drink could make a fortune.

Alcohol and crime

- Gangsters fought each other for control of the bootlegging business. The most spectacular incident was the St Valentine's Day massacre in 1929.
- The government tried to enforce the law. But it was very difficult. The police and local politicians were often bribed to turn a blind eye to the gangsters.
- The most infamous gangster was Al Capone. He made tens of millions of dollars out of Prohibition, though he spent millions on bribes.
- Although he was known to be a criminal the government could not touch him; he even made the front cover of *Time* magazine. Eventually he was imprisoned for not paying his taxes.
- Prohibition was meant to reduce lawlessness. The effect was the opposite. Ordinary citizens were willing to break the law. They did not believe in Prohibition.
- By the 1930s it was obvious that the law could not be enforced. Both Presidential candidates agreed in the 1932 election that Prohibition should end. It was abolished in 1933.

Summary box 4

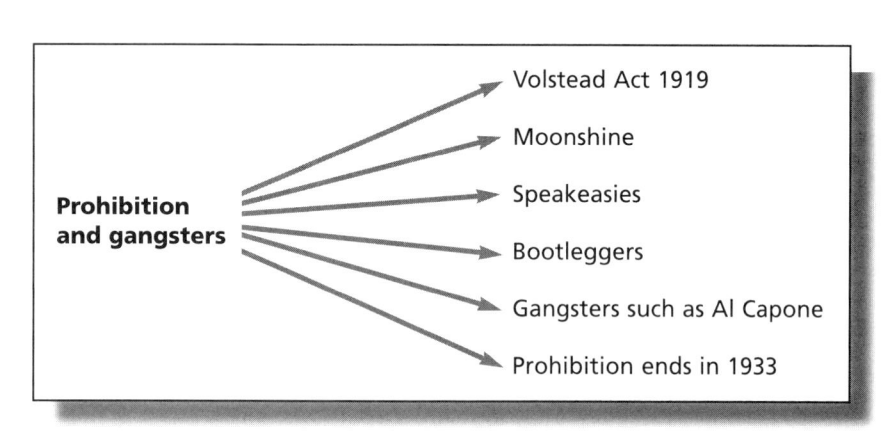

Prohibition and gangsters
- Volstead Act 1919
- Moonshine
- Speakeasies
- Bootleggers
- Gangsters such as Al Capone
- Prohibition ends in 1933

Farming

- Farming enjoyed a boom time during the First World War and many farmers borrowed to expand their farms.
- After the war Europe stopped buying American produce. Farm production and income fell, particularly in the southern states.

- The farmers worst off were the sharecroppers. They had to pay 60 per cent of their crops to the land owner. The poorest of them were the black farm workers. Many had jobs as farm labourers and when farmers struggled the black workers would lose their jobs.
- Poor white farmers blamed the new immigrants to America, they blamed the Jews and the Catholics, and they blamed the government in Washington DC. They blamed anyone they could think of.

Ku Klux Klan

- The Ku Klux Klan was a secret group of southern white people.
- The Ku Klux Klan was opposed to blacks, Catholics, Jews, liberals and liberated women. They especially believed that black people were inferior to whites. Black people therefore should not be treated, or expect to be treated, as the equals of white people. Any black people who behaved as if they were equal were punished by the Klan. This meant they could be lynched, tarred (covered in oil) or just beaten up.
- It was almost impossible to prosecute Klan members for their crimes. The Klan had links with influential members of the southern communities and had the capacity to threaten potential witnesses. Even if cases reached trial it was common to find jury members who supported the Klan.
- During the 1920s joining the Klan was often the way white farmers released their hatred at not sharing in America's boom.
- Despite their own poverty, black people were seen by southern whites as the cause of poverty. Intimidation led to the migration of thousands of black people to the northern towns. They still had the worst jobs and often lived in slums, but they suffered less racial intimidation.

Summary box 5

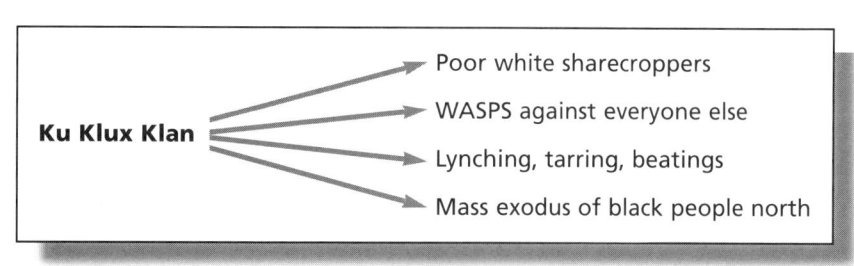

Ku Klux Klan
- Poor white sharecroppers
- WASPS against everyone else
- Lynching, tarring, beatings
- Mass exodus of black people north

Black people in America, 1918–41
In the South

- Since the time of slavery, the black people of America had been seen as second-class citizens.
- In the southern states, laws were introduced to stop them voting, as there were more black people than whites in some of these areas, and they were therefore a threat.
- Black people received very poor education. They got the worst jobs and the worst housing.

- It did seem to some that the only way to improve their life would be to return to Africa.
- Marcus Garvey set up 'Back to Africa', a movement that wanted to set up a black empire. It failed after Garvey was found to have committed fraud.

In the North

- After the First World War many black people began moving to the north.
- There were both positive and negative sides to the new life in the northern cities:

Positive
- Better jobs
- The chance of a good education
- The chance to go to university
- The chance to become middle-class
- The chance to own a business
- Jazz was very popular, good musicians earned good money

Negative
- Most black people still lived in poverty
- Black people's education was still inferior to whites
- Many white people would not allow black people into their neighbourhood
- Many black people in the north were unhappy at the number of black people arriving from the south. They felt it increased racial tensions and made it harder to get jobs.

Improvements for black people

- Life, on the whole, improved for black people, but they would never achieve any kind of equality, especially after the Depression, when it seemed there were bigger problems.
- As for much of America, it was the coming of the Second World War that helped black people more than anything else.

Summary box 6

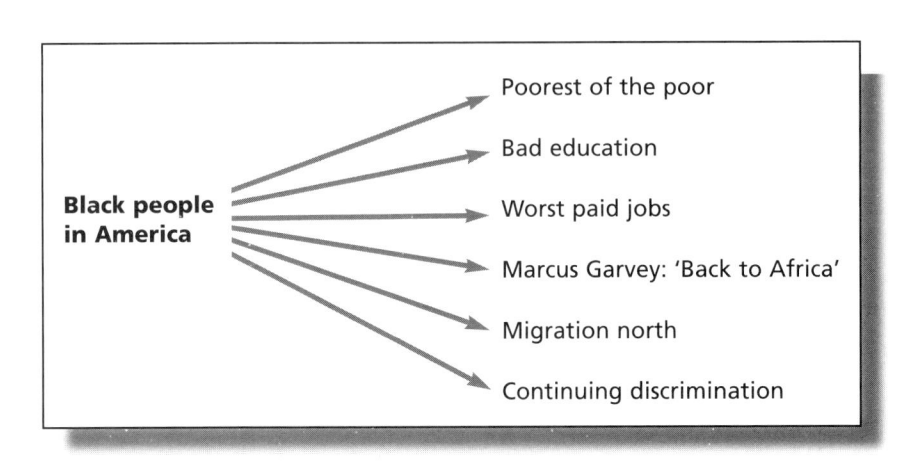

Black people in America:
- Poorest of the poor
- Bad education
- Worst paid jobs
- Marcus Garvey: 'Back to Africa'
- Migration north
- Continuing discrimination

Women in America, 1918–41

- Before the First World War, most women's lives were very restricted. They were not expected to be brash, their clothing was plain, and make-up was rare. They were expected to be housewives and, in most states, they did not have the right to vote.
- The First World War changed a lot of attitudes and winning the vote in 1920 was a major turning point.
- New labour-saving devices, such as vacuum cleaners and washing machines, helped make daily chores easier, and the car made women freer.
- Speakeasies made it easier for women to drink, smoke and wear make-up.
- More women were getting jobs, especially in the urban areas. As they became more independent, advertisers targeted them. Henry Ford's decision to expand his car colour range is thought to have been influenced by the need to attract women buyers.
- Greater independence was accompanied by more divorces.

However, not everything changed to the advantage of women.

- The work they did was paid less than men's work.
- Very few women achieved any kind of real political power, though Eleanor Roosevelt, whose husband was elected President in 1932, was said to have had great influence.

Summary box 7

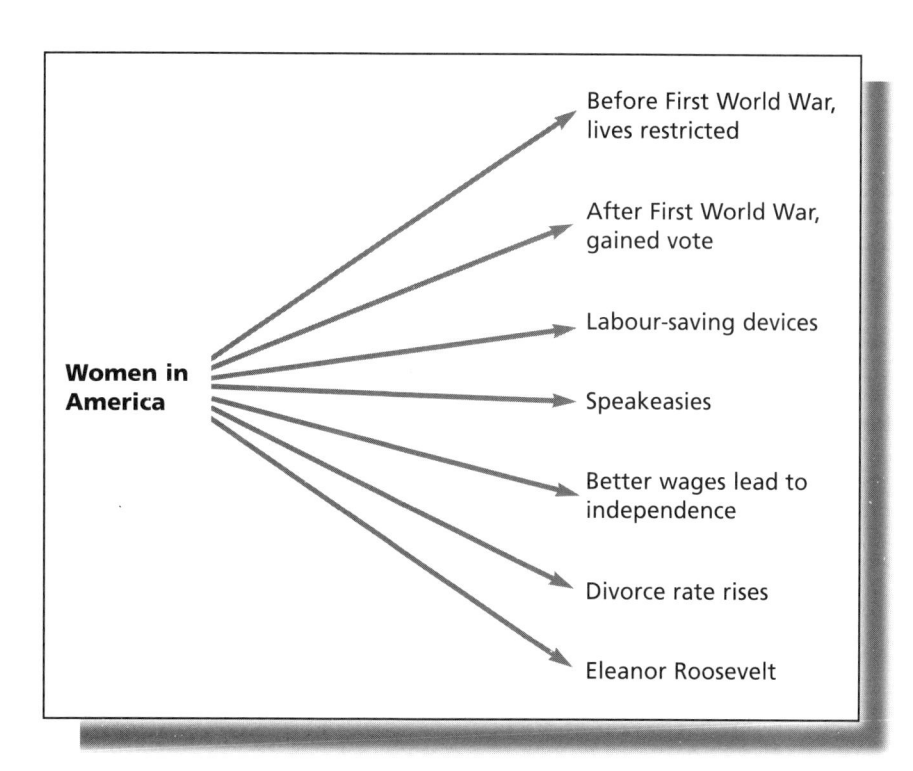

Women in America
- Before First World War, lives restricted
- After First World War, gained vote
- Labour-saving devices
- Speakeasies
- Better wages lead to independence
- Divorce rate rises
- Eleanor Roosevelt

4 What do I Know?

Once you have revised this topic thoroughly you should be able to answer most of these questions without using your notes. How many can you get right?

1. Who first introduced mass production?
2. What impact did the car industry have on other industries?
3. Which town became famous for film production?
4. How did the growth of film and radio help car sales?
5. What was Prohibition?
6. Which groups supported it most strongly?
7. What is the name of home-made alcohol?
8. What was the name of the illegal bars selling drink?
9. What was the name of the day when eight gangsters were executed in Chicago?
10. What type of music was very popular in the 1920s?
11. What is meant by the initials WASP?
12. What is the name given to covering a man in oil?
13. Name two groups the Ku Klux Klan hated.
14. In which year were women given the vote?
15. Who said 'a chicken in every pot' and 'a car in every garage'?

My score ………

What was important about:
- Mass production
- Cinema
- Al Capone
- Hire purchase?

5 Key Dates to Learn

1919	Volstead Act
1920	Women given vote
1928	Election of Herbert Hoover as President
1929	St Valentine's Day massacre
1933	Repeal of Volstead Act.

6 Exam Type Question

Here is the sort of question that you might be asked in an exam. Look at the answer given and the examiner's comments. Then answer the question yourself.

> Using the following sources and your own knowledge, explain why Prohibition led to organised crime in America. Why was it repealed in 1933? **(10 marks)**

Source A

'Prohibition is a business. All I do is supply a public demand.'

▲ Al Capone commenting on Prohibition.

The 'Boom' Years: the USA in the 1920s

Source B

> Far from making the United States free from drink, Prohibition had the opposite effect. Millions of Americans drank in illegal bars, or speakeasies, run by criminals.

▲ Written by a modern historian.

Source C

> 'Ten years ago a dishonest policeman was a rarity ... Now the honest ones are pointed out as rarities.'

▲ A comment by an American living in the 1920s.

Answer

Because ordinary Americans were willing to break the law, so the gangsters were able to make massive fortunes. As Capone said in Source A, without public demand there could not be the gangsters.

Source B says that many Americans were drinking in 'speakeasies'. As a result the speakeasies became big business. If you owned a 'speakeasy' you had to make sure that you were not closed down by the federal authorities. Soon gangsters were spending millions in bribes to make sure the police turned a blind eye, as indicated in Source C.

If you did not run the 'speakeasies', but you wanted the big profits, the only way to start in the business was to fight those already involved. The St Valentine's Day massacre is the most famous example of this, when eight of Capone's rivals were murdered on the streets of Chicago.

Despite the efforts of the authorities, Prohibition did not work. Before the change in the law there were 15,000 bars in New York, yet by 1933 there were 32,000 speakeasies in the city. Because it was illegal to buy drink, there were no laws to protect the customers. Home-made alcohol (moonshine) was often of poor quality and very expensive. The areas of the country that were more fortunate were those on the borders of Canada and Mexico where alcohol was smuggled (bootlegged) into the United States.

Eventually, the government realised that they could not stop the selling of drink. If Prohibition continued, then the only people who would benefit would be the gangsters. It was a sign of how lawless America had become when judges and police chiefs were found to be socialising with people like Capone. The repeal of Prohibition turned ordinary citizens into law-abiding people; and the gangsters were seen as criminals again by the vast majority of Americans.

Examiner's Comments

This is a good answer that covers all the main points. It uses the sources without simply copying them. The candidate has obviously revised. There are three facts not in the sources: the St Valentine's Day massacre, the number of bars in New York, and the knowledge about bootleggers. This knowledge can only be achieved by revision. Finally, the candidate sticks to the question. For example, the St Valentine's Day massacre is used as evidence of lawlessness; however the story is not retold blow by blow. To do so would be a waste of time. This answer is well on the way to a high grade. Had it been expanded to include a little more material (e.g. that only some people supported Prohibition and most did not) this would have got 8 marks out of 10.

7

Practice Question

Now answer the question yourself. Then compare your answer to the one above.

Remember that being able to answer a question that requires both use of the sources and your own knowledge means:

1 First, you must show that you understand the sources, but you must not copy them.
2 You then must show that you have knowledge that is not found in the sources, but that is of use to the question. This must be relevant to the question.

12. The Wall Street Crash

1. Topic Summary

Before 1929, it looked as if America would just get richer and richer. One sign of this was the seemingly never-ending rise in share prices. The Wall Street stock market kept rising. Shares were seen as a way of getting rich fast. Many Americans were buying shares, even those who had no idea how the stock market worked. Then the bubble burst, helping create the worst Depression in American history. Millions of people were ruined.

2. What do I Need to Know?

You will be expected to know the basic principles of shares and share dealing. You will also need to know how people were financing the purchase of shares. You will have to explain why the prices of shares fell rapidly in October 1929 and the causes and consequences of this event.

3. The Wall Street Crash

Share-buying craze

- During the 1920s many American companies were making big profits. With rising demand in America and virtually no competition from abroad, companies were selling more goods than they could make.
- This meant higher wages for the workers, more workers being employed, and big profits being given out as dividends to shareholders. It seemed the 'boom' would never end.
- There was a huge demand for the shares of these companies. Share prices rose and rose. Many sold their shares for big profits.
- As time went on more and more people wanted to make a quick profit. Buying shares seemed to be the easiest way of doing this. To do it many people borrowed huge amounts of money to buy shares, anticipating they would sell the shares before they had to pay the loan back. One of the problems was that people were buying any type of share irrespective of how well a company was doing.

But:

- By 1928-9 most Americans who could afford new consumer goods had bought them, so demand for them started to fall. As a result the profits of some companies began to fall and so their share price was bound to follow.
- Stock markets do not always go up in value. Experienced dealers knew this. Unfortunately, many of the new dealers only had experience of the good times and rising prices.

The Wall Street Crash

- During the summer of 1929, there was a 'feeling' that the price of shares had reached their peak. The price of shares started to fall slowly. When people realised what was happening they began to sell their shares. Then panic selling began as people feared they would lose their money if they didn't sell.
- Panic selling actually led to the 'expected' fall in prices. So many shares were sold that often nobody knew exactly the price of the shares until hours later.

Stock market collapses

- Black Thursday, 24 October 1929. The stock market collapsed and many thousands of people were ruined. This was the Wall Street Crash.
- The immediate effect of the crash was the ruin of the speculators, those who only bought and sold shares to make money.
- It was obvious that many people had borrowed much more from the banks than could now ever be paid back. The crash meant that banks had to call in all their loans. This ruined millions of people's lives as they had no money to pay back the loans with. They lost their homes, farms, jobs and businesses. It also ruined many banks which were unable to recover their money. Added to this were the losses many banks suffered from investing in shares themselves.
- Hoover had said, 'prosperity was just around the corner'. He could not have been more wrong. What was just around the corner was the worst economic Depression America had ever experienced.
- People who still had savings took them out of the banks, which they no longer trusted. They also decided to keep their money rather than spend it.
- With much fewer people buying goods, fewer companies could afford to pay high wages or employ as many people. This made the Depression even worse. It was a vicious circle.

Summary box 1

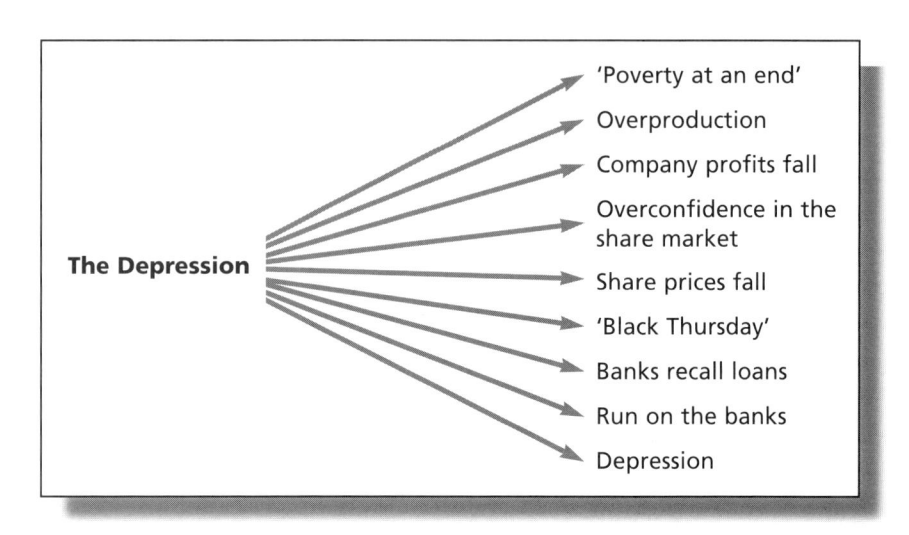

The Depression
- 'Poverty at an end'
- Overproduction
- Company profits fall
- Overconfidence in the share market
- Share prices fall
- 'Black Thursday'
- Banks recall loans
- Run on the banks
- Depression

The Wall Street Crash

Hoovervilles

- During the Depression, thousands of unemployed people roamed America in the hope of finding work.
- These people had no-where to live, so they set up shanty towns on waste land or parkland.
- The shanty towns were made up of housing put together using whatever the people could get their hands on. They had no sanitation, heating or electricity.
- Most people blamed President Hoover for the Depression. As an ironic joke the shanty towns were named 'Hoovervilles'.
- On occasions Hoover would try and force people out of the Hoovervilles; he even used troops and tear gas.
- Hoover tried to make out that these people were communists and scroungers, but the American public were not convinced. Many knew these people were decent Americans.
- Hoover and the Republican Party were seen as uncaring and heartless. A famous slogan (saying) from the time was, 'In Hoover we trusted, and now we are busted!' But the government was just following what many people at the time believed. That is, it was not the role of government to create jobs. Business had originally made America rich and it would do so again.

Task — Study the diagram of the downward spiral below. Write a paragraph explaining what it shows.

- Demand for goods drops
- Company profits fall
- Workers laid off
- Less money to buy goods
- Demand for goods drops

▲ The downward spiral of the American economy.

4

What do I Know?

Once you have revised this topic thoroughly you should be able to answer most of these questions without using your notes. How many can you get right?

1. Who was elected President in 1928?
2. What political party did he belong to?
3. Why did American companies sell more goods than they could make in the 1920s?
4. What is the name given to the share of the profits given to shareholders?
5. Where are shares bought and sold in America?
6. Why couldn't American companies in the 1920s sell many of their goods abroad?
7. Who said 'Prosperity is just around the corner'?
8. Why did share prices drop so dramatically in October 1929?
9. What is 24 October 1929 better known as?
10. What do we call it when large numbers of people take all their money out of a bank?
11. What were the shanty towns set up by the unemployed called?
12. Why didn't Hoover do more to help the unemployed?

My score ....

What was important about:
- Rising share prices
- Overproduction
- Black Thursday
- Hoovervilles?

5

Key Dates to Learn

1928	Unemployment at 1.6 million
1928	Hoover elected President
1929	Wall Street Crash
1932	Roosevelt elected President
1933	Unemployment reaches 14 million.

6

Using the Sources

The two photographs that follow contain much useful information about Roosevelt. What can we learn from these and what do they tell us about how the public can be manipulated?

Source A

◀ Roosevelt in his car shaking hands with a miner during the 1932 election campaign.

Source B

▲ Roosevelt got plenty of publicity from attending this baseball game.

The two photographs above show how, even in a democratic country, propaganda is used and people's opinions manipulated.

Source A shows Roosevelt canvassing in the 1932 election. An image of a possible future President in a wheelchair would probably not result in victory. However, put the candidate in an open-top car and this creates a totally different image. It shows a man who owns an important car, yet is willing to meet ordinary people. (The man he is shaking hands with is obviously a miner.) Unfortunately too many people see a wheelchair as meaning the occupant is not strong enough to be President. A big car represents wealth and power.

Source B shows Roosevelt appearing at the opening match of a baseball season. The image is important in certain respects. First, Roosevelt is standing unaided and he has a broad smile. Second, he is at a very important match in one of America's most popular sports. It will get plenty of exposure on television and newsreels all over the country.

As with any photographs you have to understand that they are taken for a specific reason. A photograph can convey an image to thousands of people much easier than words. The image stays in people's minds for a very long time.

The Wall Street Crash

7

Exam Type Question

In an exam you might be asked a question that involves a photograph as a source from which you have to extract information and ideas. Look at the following source and at the answers and the examiner's comments. Then answer the question yourself.

> Is there enough evidence in the source to understand the effects of the Depression on America in 1932? Use the source and your own knowledge to explain your answer. **(8 marks)**

▲ Central Park, New York 1932.

Answer 1

The source gives us a lot of useful information. We can actually see a Hooverville, so we know they did exist. We also can see the posh flats in the background, which tell us that not all Americans were poor during the Depression. We would need to have a bit more information about what was happening elsewhere in the country before we could understand the effects of the Depression, but I think that this photograph sums up a lot of what happened in the Depression.

Answer 2

> No, there is obviously not enough evidence alone in the source. We do not know what is happening in the Deep South of America, where millions of sharecroppers were forced to migrate to California to find work. The photograph cannot show us that. The photograph does not show us the soup queues, or the fights with the police. The photograph cannot tell us specific detail such as the level of unemployment, or that President Hoover was not re-elected President in 1932. Although an historian could use the source, it is not enough.

Examiner's Comments on: Answer 1

This answer is reasonable giving a general explanation of what is in the source. It has also tried to explain what is missing, but it is too general. It needs to give specific points. Examiners like to see that you know real points not just have a general understanding. This answer would get 3–4 marks.

Answer 2

This answer is better, but it does not completely answer the question. Although it shows a great deal of specific knowledge, it does the opposite of Answer 1, because it does not show any real analysis of the source itself. It needs to consider the photographer's motives. What is the reason for taking the particular picture? Is the photographer a Democrat supporter? Overall this would get 4–5 marks.

Practice Question

Now answer the question yourself. Then compare your answer with the above answers.

13. The 'New Deal'

1. Topic Summary

Following the Wall Street Crash there was widespread poverty and mass unemployment. Over the next ten years, President Roosevelt tried to solve the problems with his 'New Deal' and many of his actions were successful. Yet some historians say it was the involvement of America in the Second World War, ending it's policy of isolationism, that was to finally end the problems of the Depression.

2. What do I Need to Know?

You will need to know the details of Roosevelt's measures to try and overcome the Depression and how successful they were. You need to know who supported Roosevelt, who opposed him and why his actions caused so much controversy in America.

3. History of the New Deal

F. D. Roosevelt and the New Deal

- Although he came from a wealthy background Roosevelt was a Democrat who won the 1932 Presidential election promising a 'New Deal' to overcome the Depression. He said he was, 'waging war against … Destruction, Delay, Deceit and Despair.'
- Despite being accused by many for being both a fascist and a communist, he was supported by the American people. After 1932, Roosevelt was re-elected three more times.
- It was in his first 100 days in office that he did his most active work, producing laws to help agriculture, industry and the banks.
- His three aims were to:
  - Help those suffering from the effects of the New Deal
  - Make sure that the stock market crash could never happen again
  - Create work for the unemployed.
- Many people objected to the New Deal. These were usually people from big business and the rich who did not like paying taxes to help those in need. They felt it was not the 'American way!'
- Often these people owned the newspapers. It often seemed as if no one supported Roosevelt, until election day, when he won.
- As Roosevelt said, 'Everyone is against the New Deal except the voters.'

The 'New Deal'

Summary box 1

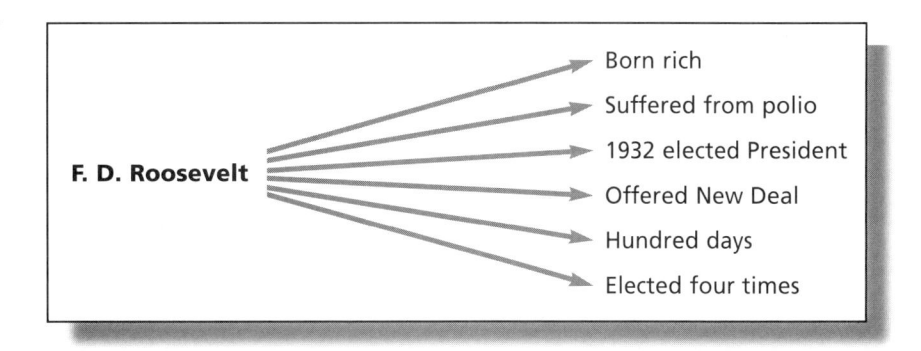

F. D. Roosevelt
- Born rich
- Suffered from polio
- 1932 elected President
- Offered New Deal
- Hundred days
- Elected four times

The hundred days

- Roosevelt said that the only thing to fear was 'fear itself'. He set about trying to solve the problems of the Depression.
- One of his first actions was to close all the banks for a few days so that government officials could inspect their books. This stopped people withdrawing their money. It gave the banks breathing space; and it stopped the panic.
- When the banks reopened people were reassured of their soundness and started depositing money in them again.
- Roosevelt then set about passing 15 new laws over the next 100 days, including ones to set up the Civilian Conservation Corps and the Tennessee Valley Authority, as well as the passing of the Agricultural Adjustment Act.
- Americans could now see that their government was trying to help. The crises were now over. Roosevelt then set about dealing with the many problems facing America in the long term.
- Not everything that Roosevelt did was a success, but he showed that he cared and that he was willing to make mistakes in trying to help.

Summary box 2

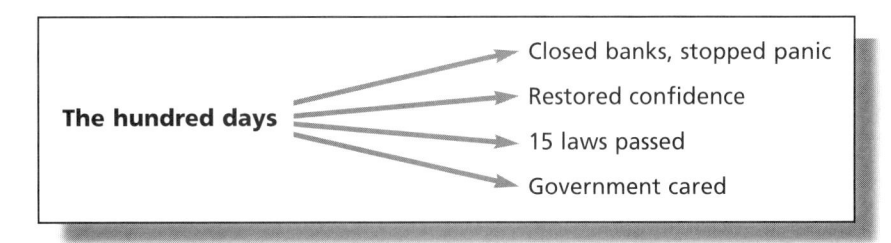

The hundred days
- Closed banks, stopped panic
- Restored confidence
- 15 laws passed
- Government cared

Fireside chats

- One way Roosevelt set about reassuring the ordinary people was through a weekly programme on the radio. Sitting by a fire in his office he spoke to the people.
- He would explain a specific policy in a simple way. He did not try to lecture to the people. In this way they felt part of the discussion and had helped with the answer.

The 'New Deal'

- In an early programme he persuaded people that the safest place for their money was in a bank. Soon most of the withdrawn money was put back into bank accounts.
- Later, when his policies were being attacked by the Supreme Court as being against the law, Roosevelt explained why they were wrong and he was right.
- It was a major form of propaganda, and today the President of the United States uses the radio and television regularly.

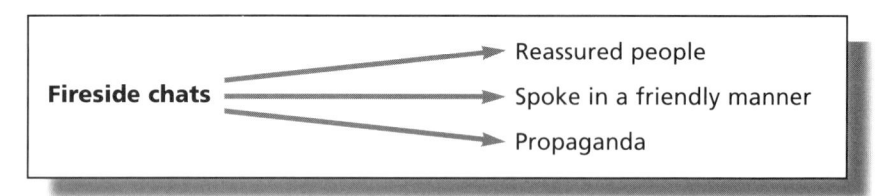

Summary box 3

```
Fireside chats ─→ Reassured people
               ─→ Spoke in a friendly manner
               ─→ Propaganda
```

The alphabet agencies

Because Roosevelt was introducing so many new laws people tried to remember them from their abbreviations. These were jokingly called the 'alphabet agencies'.

- NIRA (National Industrial Recovery Act). Workers and employers worked together to ensure that there was a minimum wage, maximum hours worked, and a set standard of quality of work. Any company that was part of the scheme could put a 'blue eagle' symbol on their product, which told the consumers that the company complied with the NIRA.
- CCC (Civilian Conservation Corps). Unemployed young men would work in the countryside helping to improve the environment. This gave them work and helped the country.
- AAA (Agricultural Adjustment Act). This limited the amount of food produced by each farmer, which limited the supply of food and as a result prices rose. If the farmer was still not earning enough the government would make up the loss. Plans were made to ensure all farms had electricity. One such scheme was the TVA.
- SSA (Social Security Act). This set up for the first time a scheme to provide pensions for the elderly, widows and the sick. It also set up unemployment benefit. Although not everyone was helped it did mean, for the first time, that the government agreed that it should help the less fortunate in society.
- WPA (Works Progress Administration). This set about providing jobs for two million people a year, building roads, bridges and schools.
- TVA (Tennessee Valley Authority). One of the poorest regions in America was Tennessee. This scheme was designed to help the region by improving it's infrastructure.
  - This was achieved by the means of placing dams all along the Tennessee River. This made sure that the river did not flood every year destroying crops and houses.

- It also meant that cheap hydro-electricity could be produced that would help the local people and attract big business into the area.
- By 1953, 93 per cent of all farms had electricity; new industries such as aluminium smelting were set up; and leisure industries on the lakes created new jobs.

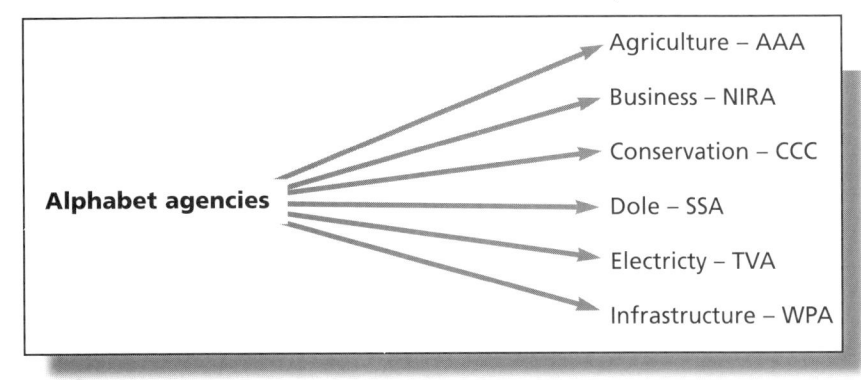

Summary box 4

Alphabet agencies:
- Agriculture – AAA
- Business – NIRA
- Conservation – CCC
- Dole – SSA
- Electricty – TVA
- Infrastructure – WPA

Opponents of the New Deal

As we have already seen, not everyone agreed with the New Deal. The four main opposing groups were:

Republicans

- Losing the 1932 election was a blow to the Republicans. They had been in power since 1920 and they felt that this was their right.
- The Republicans had always been supported in the main by the richer sections of society. They objected to the paying of higher taxes to pay for the New Deal.
- Republicans still believed in 'rugged individualism', even if they were careful to mask this in order not to look heartless, as Hoover had done prior to 1932.
- The Republicans were never to beat Roosevelt in an election and they would not regain power until after the Second World War.

Big business

- Business had suffered badly in the Wall Street Crash. However they did not approve of many of Roosevelt's policies, especially those that gave greater rights to the workers.
- Many employers, such as Henry Ford, did not recognise trade unions, yet were forced to negotiate with them on workers pay and conditions.
- Business also objected to having to help with contributions towards social security. Business believed they should be left alone to make as much profit as possible.

Supreme Court

- One way that Roosevelt's opponents tried to stop him was by saying that many of his measures were not legal. This was argued in the Supreme Court, the highest court in America.

- The nine judges of the Supreme Court declared that some of Roosevelt's agencies were unconstitutional.
- The NIRA's action to improve conditions for workers in terms of pay and conditions was seen to be against the rights of business people, who should be allowed to set their own conditions.
- Roosevelt tried to limit the powers of the 'nine old men' (as he called them) of the Supreme Court. This did not go down well as many people did not believe the President should try to influence judges, even though Roosevelt had just won a landslide victory in the 1936 Presidential election.

Radicals

- Not everyone thought that Roosevelt was going too far in his policies. Some, like Huey Long and Father C. E. Coughlin, expected more radical solutions. They wanted Roosevelt to tax the rich more and help the poor more.
- Long, Governor of Louisiana, even suggested giving every American family $6,000 to spend in order to boost the economy. To pay for this he demanded the confiscation of all fortunes over $5 million. Long was assassinated in 1935.

Summary box 5

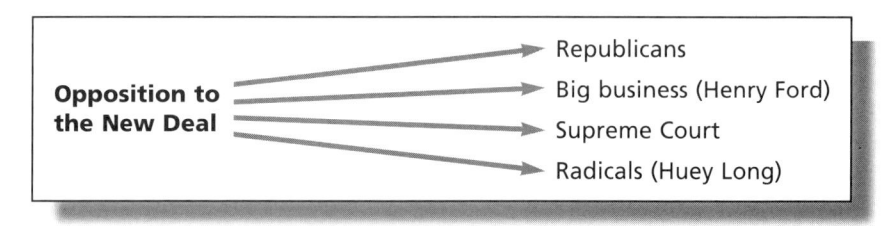

Opposition to the New Deal →
- Republicans
- Big business (Henry Ford)
- Supreme Court
- Radicals (Huey Long)

Was the New Deal a success?

- Roosevelt's policies showed that he cared and he was trying to do something. The problem was that the policies were not always as effective as first thought.
- Historians today are divided on this point. Some say that the only policy that had a lasting effect was the TVA. These historians are quick to point out that unemployment stayed high throughout the 1930s.
- This, of course, misses the whole point. Roosevelt was not a dictator like Hitler or Stalin. He did not have the powers needed to end unemployment. All he could do was make sure that the suffering was not too bad, and to ensure that he created the right environment in which a recovery could be achieved.

The effect of the Second World War

- The end of the Depression and the fall in unemployment mainly came about through the build-up to the Second World War.
- In 1939 Britain and France began buying more and more weapons in order to fight the Germans
- Roosevelt started a land lease policy. This helped boost American industry and farming.

- Despite America's isolationist policies, Roosevelt realised that at some point America would become involved in the war.
- The recruiting of soldiers, the provision of armaments and uniforms, and the investment in new technologies would soon reduce unemployment and increase prosperity.

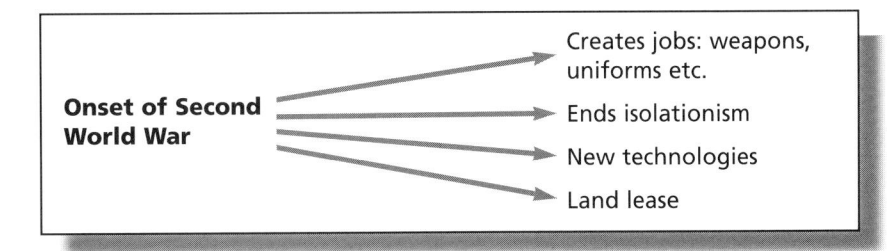

Summary box 6

Onset of Second World War
- Creates jobs: weapons, uniforms etc.
- Ends isolationism
- New technologies
- Land lease

4

What do I Know?

Once you have revised this topic thoroughly you should be able to answer most of these questions without using your notes. How many can you get right?

1. Which political party did Roosevelt belong to?
2. How many times was Roosevelt elected President?
3. What did Roosevelt say Americans had to fear?
4. Who believed in 'rugged individualism'?
5. What do we call the first few months of his first term as President?
6. How many laws were passed in those early months?
7. What was the name given to his talks on the radio to the American people?
8. What do the initials TVA stand for?
9. What do the initials NIRA stand for?
10. Name one businessman who opposed Roosevelt.
11. Name one radical who opposed Roosevelt.
12. 'Everyone is against the New Deal except ...'. Who?
13. What is the highest court in the land?
14. When did America enter the Second World War?
15. When did Roosevelt die?

My score ....

What was important about:
- Fireside chats
- The hundred days
- Relief, Recovery, Reform
- The alphabet agencies?

5

Key Dates to Learn

1932	Roosevelt elected President
1933	Hundred days
1936	Roosevelt elected for second term
1937	Defeat by Supreme Court
1940	Roosevelt elected for the third term
1941	Pearl Harbor, America enters Second World War
1944	Roosevelt elected for fourth term
1945	Roosevelt dies.

The 'New Deal'

6. Key Facts

President	Political Party	Election Date	Events
Woodrow Wilson	Democrat	1912	
Woodrow Wilson	Democrat	1916	First World War
Warren Harding	Republican	1920	
Calvin Coolridge	Republican	1924	Boom time and Prohibition
Herbert Hoover	Republican	1928	Wall Street Crash
Franklin Roosevelt	Democrat	1932	New Deal
Franklin Roosevelt	Democrat	1936	New Deal II
Franklin Roosevelt	Democrat	1940	Second World War
Franklin Roosevelt	Democrat	1944	

7. Using the Sources

Look at Sources A and B and answer the questions.

Source A

The placing of dams all along the Tennessee River made sure that the river did not flood.

This allowed the **farmers to invest more**. Farms would now always have enough water in the summer months.

Farmers could employ more workers, which in turn helped the local economy.

The dams provided a cheap supply of **hydro-electric power**.

This electricity provided cheap energy for the farmers and local people, making them better off.

The cheap electricity attracted new industries into the area. These employed more people, which boosted the local economy.

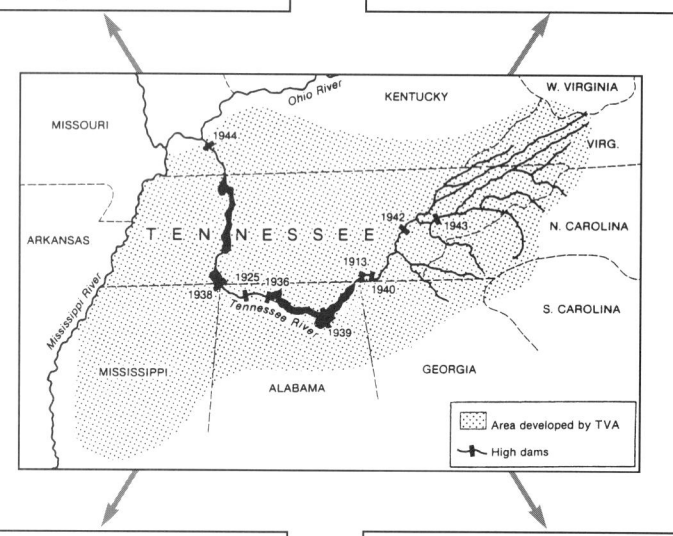

In controlling the river, the TVA created over 600 miles of **navigable waterways**. This allowed businesses to transport their goods in and out of the region very easily.

This helped to attract more businesses into the region, creating more jobs.

The scheme also created a major **leisure industry** based around watersports.

This created many jobs in the tourist industry. It also attracted people into an area that previously was considered to be poor and backward.

▲ Map of the Tennessee Valley Authority scheme and indications of the benefits that it brought to local areas.

The 'New Deal'

Source B

▲ This photograph shows the contrast between the advertisers vision and the reality for the many black people who were unemployed. Here they are queuing for government relief.

> 1 In Source A give one reason for why each factor (written in bold) helped create long-term jobs in the areas surrounding the Tennessee river.
>
> 2 In Source B
>   (a) What is being advertised? What does this mean?
>   (b) Why are the people in the queue?
>   (c) Why do you think the photographer took this photograph? What is he trying to say?

7

Exam Type Question

You will often find that there will be exam questions that involve cartoons as sources from which you have to extract information and ideas. Look at the cartoon on page 110 and the answers to this question and the examiner's comments. Then answer the question yourself.

> Look at the cartoon that follows. How reliable is this cartoon to an historian studying the 1932 Presidential election? Give reasons for your answer. **(8 marks)**

109

The 'New Deal'

▲ This cartoon shows Roosevelt getting rid of the previous government's policies, which are seen as rubbish.

Answer 1

The cartoon is not very reliable because it is from the cartoonist's point of view and he is bound to be biased. A cartoonist is paid to give his opinion. The cartoonist has drawn Roosevelt as a strong man, which he was not, as he suffered from polio. The cartoonist is obviously in favour of Roosevelt.

An historian would need to find a cartoonist from the time who was not a supporter of Roosevelt, and see what he had drawn to give a more balanced answer.

Answer 2

The cartoon reflects much of what was felt about the Presidential election of 1932. Hoover was seen as a President who had run out of new ideas. His old ideas were now shown as no good. They were rubbish. Roosevelt on the other hand had new policies and was getting rid of the rubbish — the old ideas.

Notice how Roosevelt is shown with his sleeves rolled up. This means he is willing to do some real hard work. This shows that the government will do something to help the people. This suggests that the cartoon is fairly reliable. The American people were to re-elect Roosevelt three times, so they must have liked his policies, and not those of the Republicans.

From this point of view the cartoon is very reliable, but the cartoonist might be a Democrat supporter. They might work for a Democrat newspaper. We would need to study these things before we could be assured that the cartoonist was not totally biased. At the same time we must realise that cartoonists are meant to give their opinion and not try to be balanced.

The 'New Deal'

Examiner's Comments on: Answer 1

This answer has some good points but generally it is too superficial. It does show that the candidate understands some of the imagery from the cartoon, saying that Roosevelt was strong. It also points out that the cartoon is someone's opinion, the cartoonist. Unfortunately, it does not fully develop the ideas and begins to be too general in the end. This would get 3 marks.

Answer 2

This answer is excellent, because it uses background knowledge to show how correct the source is. This is an excellent technique if you are looking at reliability, rather than just saying the source is biased because it is a cartoon. The suggestion is made that the cartoon might be by a Democrat, though a little more use of information in the source to prove this would have helped. I would give this answer 7 marks.

Practice Question

Look carefully at Sources A and B and the notes on them. Then go on to answer the question on Sources C and D.

Remember, reliability is all about trust. You need to find out who produced the source, when and why? You also need to look at the intended audience.

A cartoon is a good way for an historian to gauge public opinion. This does not mean that it is the opinion of everybody in the country, only that it represents a body of opinion within the country. Cartoons are printed in newspapers, and as such they reflect the views of many of the readers of the paper. Cartoons are a form of propaganda. This means they give greater emphasis to the good points of the cartoonist's viewpoint and/or greater emphasis to the bad points of the opposing viewpoint.

Source A

DON'T SEND MY BOYS TO PRISON

◀ Roosevelt pleading with the Supreme Court.

111

The 'New Deal'

Source B

▲ The money wasted by the New Deal.

In Source A, notice how the New Deal supporters are shown as a series of clowns and criminals. Roosevelt is shown as an old woman who cannot control her children, but protects them all the same.

In Cartoon B, Roosevelt is shown as someone who is working hard, but beneath the surface a great deal of money, and therefore Roosevelt's effort, is being wasted. You will notice that both Sources A and B do not attack Roosevelt the man, but they suggest that he does not really understand what he is doing. Roosevelt was too popular with the voters to attack him directly.

The 'New Deal'

> Look at Sources C and D and try and work out their hidden messages and the images used.

Source C

▲ Two businessmen crying over the cost of the New Deal.

Source D

▲ This cartoon shows that only two states did not vote for Roosevelt in the 1936 election.

113

Russia and the Soviet Union, 1904–54

14. Russia in Crisis, 1904–17

1. Topic Summary

Russia at the beginning of the century was a huge, backward country under the autocratic rule of the Romanov family. Political opposition to the Tsar was ruthlessly suppressed and there were few rights for the peasants of Russia, who made up almost 80 per cent of the population. During this time revolutionary groups developed and the Tsar was forced to make political concessions after an unsuccessful revolution in 1905. These concessions were soon withdrawn, however, and the Tsar continued to rule as an autocrat. When Russia went to war in 1914 it created such problems within the country that by the spring of 1917 the Tsar was close to being overthrown.

2. What do I Need to Know?

The key question in this section is 'Why did the Tsar lose control?' You will have to explain why the Romanovs went from almost total control in 1900 to being overthrown in 1917. To do this you have to know about the inequalities in the country, the opposition which developed, the Tsar's poor government and the effects of the First World War.

3. History of Russia, 1904–17

Russia in 1904

- Russia was a huge, but underdeveloped country. It's peasants often faced starvation and its industrial workers lived and worked in terrible conditions.
- Of the 125 million people who lived in Russia, few had any say in how it was run. The Tsar and the nobility (about 1% of the population) had almost all the wealth and all the political power.
- The Tsar had complete control of how the country was run. He appointed a Committee of Ministers to help him govern and had a secret police, the Okhrana, to deal with any opposition. Yet Tsar Nicholas (1904-17) was not an able leader and made many mistakes during his reign.
- The Tsar was also supported by the Russian Orthodox Church, whose priests taught that it was a sin to oppose the Tsar.
- Despite the lack of political freedoms and their poor living conditions many of the Russian people adored the Tsar and believed that their problems were caused by him selecting 'poor ministers'.

Opposition to the Tsar

Nicholas's grandfather, Alexander II, had been assassinated in 1881, so Nicholas was careful to clamp down on opponents, but despite this, three main groups of opposition developed.

- **The Liberals**. These were mostly educated middle-class Russians who wanted their country to become a democracy like other European powers.
- **The Social Revolutionaries**. These were a radical group who wanted Russia's land divided amongst the peasants, not kept by wealthy landowners.
- **The Social Democratic Party**. This based its views on Karl Marx. It wanted factory workers to help set up a socialist, and eventually communist, system in Russia. This party later divided into Mensheviks and Bolsheviks.

Summary box 1

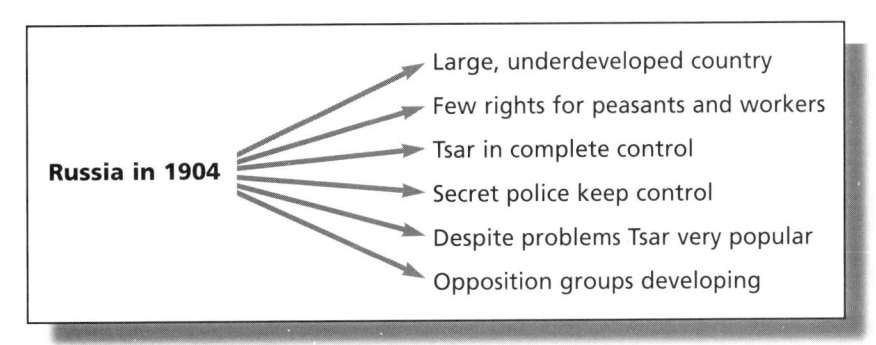

Russia in 1904:
- Large, underdeveloped country
- Few rights for peasants and workers
- Tsar in complete control
- Secret police keep control
- Despite problems Tsar very popular
- Opposition groups developing

How Marx thought Russia would become Communist

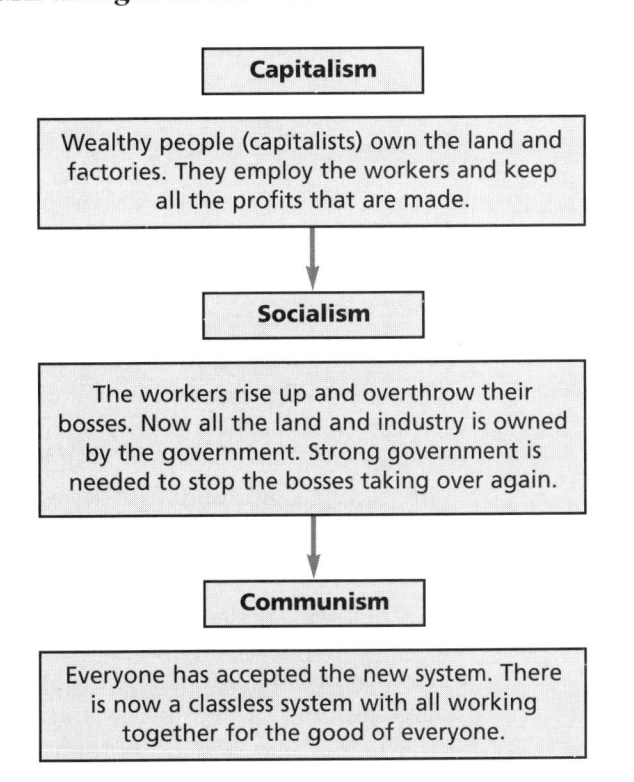

Capitalism
Wealthy people (capitalists) own the land and factories. They employ the workers and keep all the profits that are made.

↓

Socialism
The workers rise up and overthrow their bosses. Now all the land and industry is owned by the government. Strong government is needed to stop the bosses taking over again.

↓

Communism
Everyone has accepted the new system. There is now a classless system with all working together for the good of everyone.

Dress rehearsal? – the revolution of 1905

- The years 1900–4 saw bad harvests and inflation. There were many strikes and the Minister of the Interior was assassinated. In 1904 his replacement, Plehve, was also killed.
- In 1904–5 the Russians fought a war against the Japanese. They were easily defeated and returning soldiers told stories of incompetent leaders and poor supplies at the front.
- On Sunday 22 January 1905 Father Gapon led 200,000 workers to the Tsar's Winter Palace to hand in a petition. The Tsar was not there but his troops fired on the demonstrators. Official figures say 96 people were killed, but the numbers were probably much higher. This became known as 'Bloody Sunday'.
- There was strong reaction to the events of Bloody Sunday. Half-a-million workers went on strike and the Tsar's uncle, Sergei Alekandrovich, was assassinated.
- In May 1905 the unions of Russia joined together to form the Union of Unions.
- In June the crew of the battleship *Potemkin* mutinied.
- In St Petersburg there was a general strike and a council, or Soviet, was formed to organise the strike.

Summary box 2

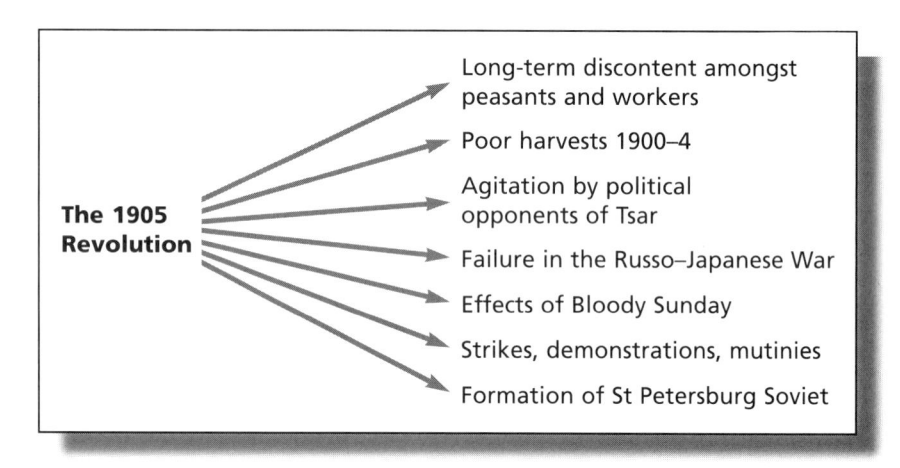

The 1905 Revolution
- Long-term discontent amongst peasants and workers
- Poor harvests 1900–4
- Agitation by political opponents of Tsar
- Failure in the Russo–Japanese War
- Effects of Bloody Sunday
- Strikes, demonstrations, mutinies
- Formation of St Petersburg Soviet

Concessions

Nicholas's Chief Minister, Sergei Witte, persuaded the Tsar that to restore his control he had to make concessions.
- These came in the October Manifesto when Nicholas agreed to set up a parliament (Duma), allow all Russians to vote, and allow the setting up of political parties and freedom of speech.

Reprisals

The concessions soon turned out to be little more than a move to buy time. Reprisals soon began.
- Groups of landowners and other government supporters set up organisations, called 'Black Hundreds', to murder opponents of the Tsar. The police did nothing to stop them.

- In 1906 the Tsar issued the Fundamental Laws giving him complete control over the Duma. In the same year he dismissed Witte and appointed the more hard-lined Stolypin. There were four Dumas between 1905 and 1917. Two were dismissed by Nicholas for asking for reforms. The last two survived longer because they knew 'how to behave'.
- Early in 1906 the Social Revolutionaries had begun a campaign of terrorism to show that the Tsar could not keep control. Stolypin set up special courts to deal with this. Over a thousand terrorists were executed and 20,000 sent into exile. Stolypin also reduced opposition to the Tsar by setting up schemes to help peasants buy the land they farmed.
- By 1910 the numbers of revolutionaries in Russia had declined from 100,000 to 10,000.

Summary box 3

From revolution to war:
- October Manifesto – concessions made
- Fundamental Laws undermine concessions
- Social Revolutionaries carry out terrorism
- Black Hundreds attack Tsar's opponents
- Stolypin cracks down on opposition
- Some reform to help peasants

The impact of the war

By 1914 it seemed that the Tsar had regained control. But Russia's poor showing in the First World War soon changed the situation.

- In 1914 Russia joined Britain and France against Germany, Austria-Hungary and Turkey. Russian forces won early victories but soon lost hundreds of thousands of men at the battles of Tannenberg and Masurian Lakes.
- By the end of 1914 Russian casualties were over one million and the Germans and Austrians had advanced more than 300 miles (480 km) into Russia.
- In 1915 the Tsar went to the Front and took personal control of the war. This was unwise because:
  - Now he could be blamed for everything that went wrong – and plenty did! For example, in 1916 the Tsar ordered an attack on the Germans that resulted in the death of one million of his soldiers.

- His presence at the Front left his (German) wife in control at home. She allowed Rasputin to have a major say in how Russia was run. Rasputin was so corrupt that the Tsar's government became even more unpopular. In the end Rasputin was assassinated by a royal prince!
- The war had a devastating effect on Russia. Millions of men were killed, prices rocketed (in 1917 things cost seven times what they had in 1914) and there were shortages of food and raw materials at home.

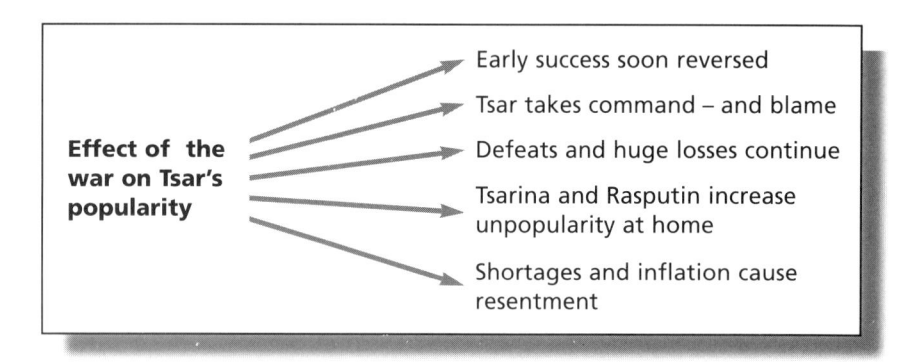

Summary box 4

Effect of the war on Tsar's popularity
- Early success soon reversed
- Tsar takes command – and blame
- Defeats and huge losses continue
- Tsarina and Rasputin increase unpopularity at home
- Shortages and inflation cause resentment

The end of Tsarist government

The Tsar's government was eventually overthrown, not by some great plan, but perhaps because of cold weather!

- The winter of 1916–17 was extremely cold and this reinforced discontent that already existed about food and fuel shortages.
- In the capital, Petrograd (its name had been changed from St Petersburg, which sounded too German), there were strikes and demonstrations as food began to run out. On 9 March 1917 200,000 demonstrators called for the overthrow of the Tsar.
- The government had placed 340,000 troops in the city in case of riots. On 11 March Nicholas ordered their commander to restore order, but many of the troops were young recruits who were not happy about firing on their fellow citizens.
- The President of the Duma, Rodzyanko, told Nicholas that he needed to form a new government with the support of the people. Nicholas replied 'That fat Rodzyanko has again sent me some nonsense to which I will not even reply.'
- On 12 March the soldiers in Petrograd began deserting and soon the city was in the hands of revolutionaries. Twelve members of the Duma formed a Provisional Government led by Prince Lvov.
- Nicholas decided to return to Petrograd, but was told that his rule was over. He agreed to abdicate in favour of his cousin, Grand Duke Michael. But Michael would only take over if the Provisional Government supported him. It did not.

The rule of the Romanovs had come to an end.

Russia in Crisis, 1904–17

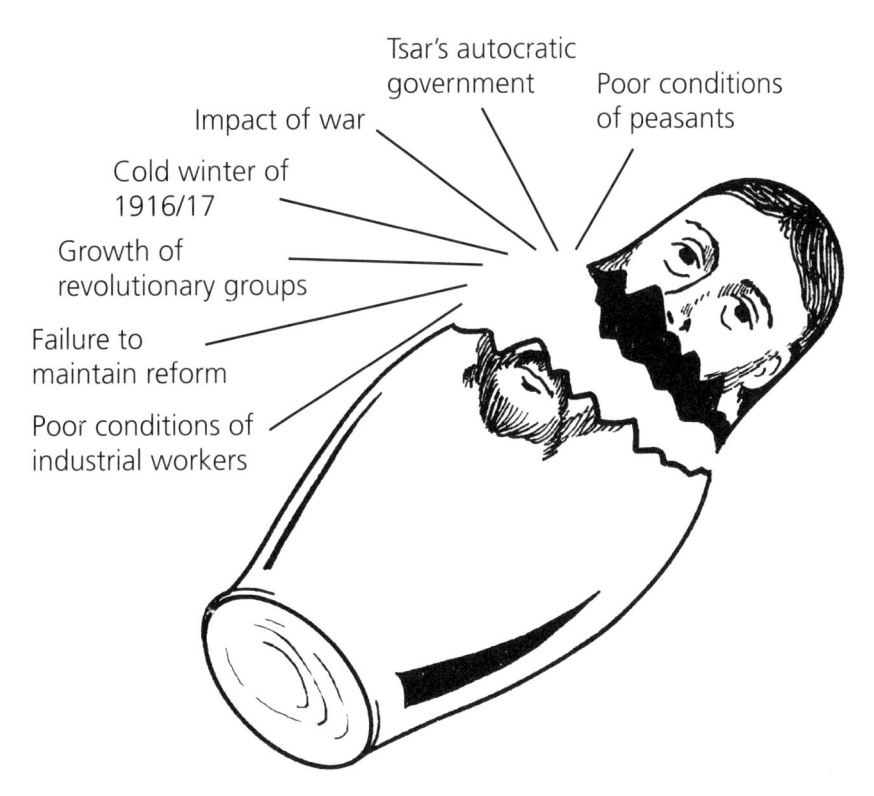

Summary box 5

Reasons for the fall of the Tsar.

- Tsar's autocratic government
- Poor conditions of peasants
- Impact of war
- Cold winter of 1916/17
- Growth of revolutionary groups
- Failure to maintain reform
- Poor conditions of industrial workers

4

What do I Know?

Once you have revised this topic thoroughly you should be able to answer most of these questions without using your notes. How many can you get right?

1. What percentage of the Russian population were peasants?
2. What was the Church in Russia called?
3. What was the name of the Russian secret police?
4. Which group did Nicholas select to help him govern?
5. What did the 'Liberals' want Russia to be like?
6. Whose beliefs did the Social Revolutionaries follow?
7. Which war did the Russians lose in 1905?
8. Who led the demonstrators on Bloody Sunday?
9. What was a Duma?
10. What were Black Hundreds?
11. Who set up special courts in 1906 to deal with opposition to the Tsar?
12. Name one major defeat for Russia in the First World War.
13. Who helped the Tsarina rule whilst Nicholas was at the Front?
14. Who did Nicholas want to replace him?
15. Who took over the government of Russia in March 1917?

My score ....

What was importance of:
- Karl Marx
- Bloody Sunday
- The Fundamental Laws
- Rasputin?

119

Russia in Crisis, 1904–17

5 Exam Type Question

Not surprisingly, a common question for you to answer is why the Tsar's government was overthrown. Here is an example.

> How far do Sources A and B explain why the Tsar was overthrown in March 1917? **(12 marks)**

Source A

I must give you a message from Rasputin, prompted by what he saw in the night. He begs you to order an advance near Riga, otherwise the Germans will settle down through all the winter. He says we can and we must, and I was to write to you at once.

▲ From a letter from Alexandra to Tsar Nicholas.

Source B

	1914	1915	1916	1917
% of working men in army	14.9	25.9	35.7	36.7
Grain production in poods	3509	4006	3319	3185
Price of goods (where 1913 = 100)	130	155	300	755

Answer 1

I think these sources are very good for explaining why the Tsar was overthrown. You can see in Source A that Rasputin has a lot of influence with the Tsarina – and he is even telling the Tsar how to fight the war (because he saw it in the night in a dream!). I know that one of the reasons why Nicholas became unpopular was because of Rasputin.

Source B also provides good evidence. The First World War was incredibly unpopular in Russia. You can see that the war meant that over a third of men were in the army and grain production dropped. You can also see that prices went up. All these things help explain why the Tsar was overthrown.

Answer 2

These sources don't provide the whole answer. Source A is good for showing the sort of poor government which took place and made the Tsar even more unpopular. Fancy Rasputin telling the Tsar what to do because he saw it in a dream. Source B is also good for showing the effects of the First World War. Obviously with so many men away the crops are not going to get planted and production is going to fall. This meant that people would starve – which would hardly have made the Tsar popular.

But there are also a lot of things the sources don't tell us. There is nothing about the way that Russia is governed so that all the power is in the hands of the Tsar. The sources don't tell you about the revolutionary groups and the revolution of 1905, or the concessions that Nicholas made in the October Manifesto but went back on. Of course you also need to know about what happened in early 1917 which turned the unpopularity of the Tsar into his final overthrow.

Examiner's Comments on: Answer 1

This answer is fine as far as it goes and uses information from the sources to explain why the Tsar was overthrown. But it doesn't address the 'How far?' part of the question by looking at ways in which the sources don't provide all we need to know. For this reason it would get only 5-6 marks.

Answer 2

This is an excellent answer. There are one or two causes missing and we might have had a little more detail, especially about the events of 1917, but it recognises how Sources A and B help, and also what else needs to be discussed to explain the Tsar's downfall. I would give it 10-11 marks.

15. The Bolshevik Victory

1. Topic Summary

The Provisional Government which took office in March 1917 was itself overthrown in October 1917 by the Bolsheviks, who had gained control of the Social Democratic Party. The Bolsheviks themselves faced fierce opposition from supporters of the Tsar and other 'Whites'. It was only after a bitter civil war and tough measures by Lenin that Russia finally emerged as the communist Soviet Union.

2. What do I Need to Know?

The most important question to answer in this section is 'Why and how did the Bolsheviks establish themselves in power by 1924?' To answer that you will need to know why the Provisional Government was overthrown, why there was a second revolution in November 1917, and how the Bolsheviks managed to defeat their opponents in the civil war. You will also need to explain who the key figures were in the Bolshevik Party and what part they played in events between 1917 and 1924.

3. History of the Bolshevik Victory

The Provisional Government

In March 1917 the Provisional Government took office and Alexander Kerensky took over as leader from Prince Lvov. The new government had serious problems to deal with.

- In Petrograd the real power lay in the hands of the Soviet, which had been formed in March 1917. Since Kerensky was a leading member of the Soviet, the Provisional Government was supported at first, but soon lost that support.
- The Provisional Government also had the problem of what to do about the war. It decided to fight on, but this made it very unpopular. Another offensive in the summer of 1917 failed and troops began to desert in their thousands.
- The government also faced the problem of what reforms to make. Many Russians, especially the peasants, wanted immediate change. The government did introduce measures, such as freedom of speech and freeing political prisoners, but these just gave its opponents a greater voice.
- As regards land reform, the government decided to wait until a 'Constituent Assembly' was elected in November and then address the issue.
- With the overthrow of the Tsar, many of his opponents, who had been in exile, returned home. Men such as Lenin, Stalin, Trotsky and Zinoviev issued anti-government propaganda and called for 'Peace, Land and Bread'. Support for these Bolsheviks grew rapidly.

The Bolshevik Victory

- In July 1917 there was a major strike in Petrograd and in the 'July Days' thousands of Russians demanded that a Bolshevik government be set up. The Bolsheviks had not planned this and were not ready. Kerensky arrested hundreds of Bolsheviks and their leader, Lenin, fled to Finland.
- Kerensky appointed Kornilov as supreme commander of the army, but he tried to overthrow the government in September and had to be arrested.

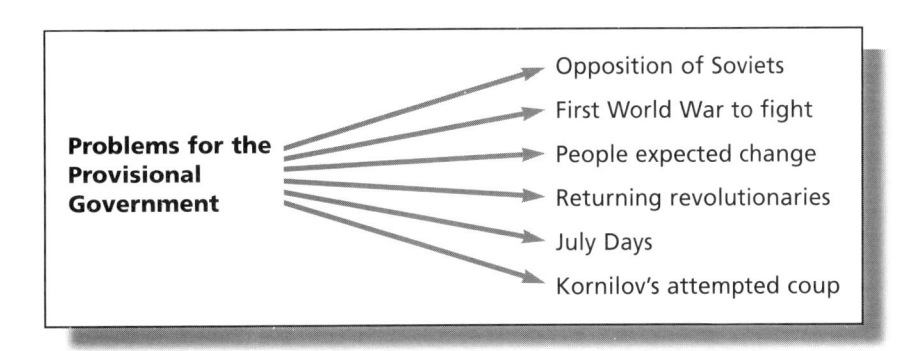

Summary box 1

Problems for the Provisional Government
- Opposition of Soviets
- First World War to fight
- People expected change
- Returning revolutionaries
- July Days
- Kornilov's attempted coup

The Bolsheviks seize power

- When Kornilov attempted his coup the Provisional Government gave the Bolsheviks weapons to help stop him. In October 1917 Lenin returned and ordered the Bolsheviks to prepare for takeover.
- In early November, while the Congress of Soviets (an organisation of the Soviets of Russia) was meeting, the Bolsheviks moved the warship *Aurora* up the River Neva to opposite the Winter Palace. Their supporters seized key points in the city and on 8 November announced that the Provisional Government had been deposed.
- Kerensky escaped from Petrograd and tried, unsuccessfully, to raise troops to defeat the Bolsheviks.

Bolshevik policies

The Bolsheviks had control of Petrograd, but this was only a small part of Russia.

They now had to follow policies that made sure that they stayed in power. To make sure that the Bolshevik policies were obeyed throughout Russia they sent details of their decrees to all the towns, cities and villages.

- The first of these was a land reform decree taking land away from nobles, the Church and landowners and sharing it amongst the peasants. Other decrees limited factory working hours to a maximum eight a day, banned religious teaching and stated that women and men were equal. All titles except 'Comrade' and 'Citizen' were banned.

- Troops were also sent into the countryside to seize grain to end food shortages in the towns.
- Elections were held straight away for the Constituent Assembly proposed by the Provisional Assembly. Since the Bolsheviks won only 175 of the 707 seats Lenin allowed it to meet only once and instead used the Congress of Soviets (with a Bolshevik majority) as the supreme governing body.
- A new secret police, the Cheka, was used to stamp out opposition. In 1918 it began a 'Red Terror', which resulted in 200,000 deaths and 85,000 Russians being imprisoned in concentration camps.
- The Bolsheviks were forced to fight a civil war against their opponents. Lenin knew that they could not do this as well as fight in the First World War against Germany and its allies. He therefore sent Trotsky to negotiate terms to get Russia out of the war. The terms of the Treaty of Brest-Litovsk were incredibly harsh. Russia lost:
  - 25% of its land
  - 80% of its coalmines
  - 50% of its industry
  - 26 % of its population
  - 26% of its railways.

Lenin, however, was determined to get peace at any price. He believed that both the Tsar and the Provisional Government had been brought down by the problems caused by the First World War.

Summary box 2

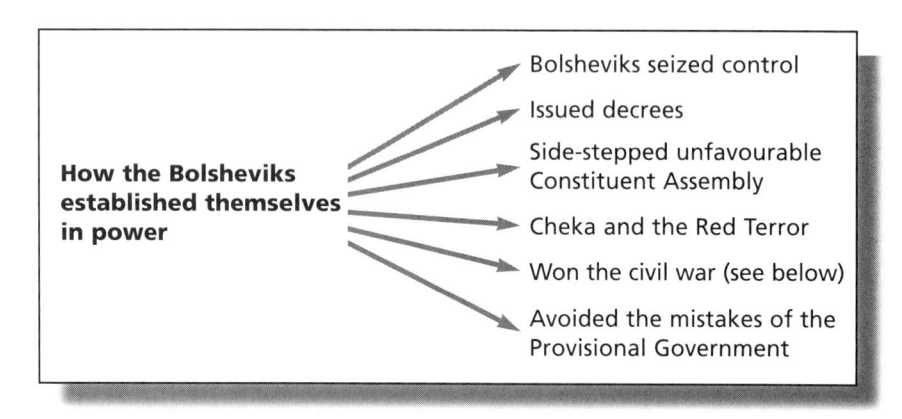

How the Bolsheviks established themselves in power
- Bolsheviks seized control
- Issued decrees
- Side-stepped unfavourable Constituent Assembly
- Cheka and the Red Terror
- Won the civil war (see below)
- Avoided the mistakes of the Provisional Government

Winning the civil war

The success of the new government depended upon its ability to defend itself against its opponents. This it had to do in the civil war from 1918 to 1921.

- The Bolshevik army was organised by Trotsky. He built a Red Army with volunteers and introduced conscription for all males aged 18–40. Many of the officers he used were captured from his opponents (whose families faced death if they refused). He also appointed commissars to ensure that strict discipline was enforced.

- The Bolsheviks' opponents, the Whites, were a disunited and poorly led group. They included supporters of the Tsar, supporters of the Provisional Government, groups trying to break free from Russian control (e.g. the Ukrainians), and expeditions sent by foreign powers, such as Britain and France, to prevent a Bolshevik government becoming established.
- In order to win the war Lenin adopted a policy of war communism. The government took control of all factories, banned private trading and rationed food. This ensured that there was enough supplies for the Red Army.
- However, war communism was very unpopular and led to food shortages and unrest in the countryside. In 1921 sailors at Kronstadt mutinied.
- Lenin realised that the policy had to change and in 1921 introduced the New Economic Policy in which small businesses were encouraged and peasants allowed to sell surplus stock. Many Bolsheviks saw the NEP as a betrayal of their principles, but Lenin was convinced that it was necessary.
- The Bolsheviks also made skillful use of propaganda to portray the Whites as supported by 'foreigners'. Support for the Red Army was support for Russia.
- The Red Army proved highly effective and by the end of 1921 the war was won.

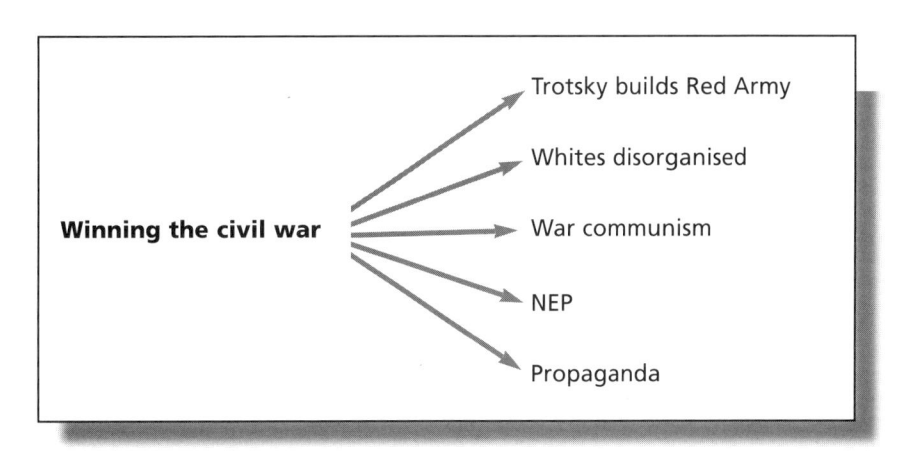

Summary box 3

Winning the civil war:
- Trotsky builds Red Army
- Whites disorganised
- War communism
- NEP
- Propaganda

The end of Tsarist Russia

- The Romanov family did not survive the civil war. In 1918 Tsar Nicholas and his family were shot in Ekaterinburg by Red forces as the town came under attack by White forces.
- In 1924 the name of the country was changed to the Union of Soviet Socialist Republics. The four republics were Russia, the Ukraine, the Caucusus and Byelorussia, though the real power lay in the hands of the Communist Party (as the Bolsheviks now called themselves) in Moscow.

The Bolshevik Victory

4. What do I Know?

Once you have revised this topic thoroughly you should be able to answer most of these questions without using your notes. How many can you get right?

1. Who took over the leadership of the Provisional Government from Kerensky?
2. What new body did the Provisional Government decide to set up?
3. Give one reason why the Provisional Government was unpopular with the people.
4. Why did some of the Provisional Government's policies help its opponents?
5. What slogan did the Bolsheviks have?
6. What were the 'July Days'?
7. Which army commander tried to carry out a coup in September 1917?
8. On what date did the Bolsheviks announce that the Provisional Government had been deposed?
9. Which treaty took Russia out of the First World War?
10. Why was this treaty criticised by many Russians?
11. Who organised the Red Army?
12. Where did many of the officers for the Red Army come from?
13. What was war communism?
14. Where was there a naval mutiny against the Bolsheviks in 1921?
15. What new name was given to Russia in 1924?

My score ………

What was important about:
- The Treaty of Brest-Litovsk
- Trotsky's work with the Red Army
- The Cheka
- The New Economic Policy?

5. Exam Type Question

This is the sort of question that is often asked in exams. Look at the attempts to answer it and the examiner's comments

How useful is the following source for someone studying the work of Lenin in Russia? **(10 marks)**

'Of all the tyrannies in history, the Bolshevik tyranny is the worst, the most destructive, the most degrading. The atrocities that were committed under Lenin and Trotsky are incomparably more hideous and more numerous than anything which the Kaiser of Germany committed.'

▲ **A comment by Winston Churchill. At the time he was British Secretary for War and Air.**

Answer 1

This would not be a very good source to use because it is biased. Winston Churchill was British and so he did not like the Bolsheviks. So what he says about Lenin is not going to be true.

Answer 2

This source is quite useful because it tells me that Lenin behaved like a tyrant. I suppose this must be referring to things such as his use of the Cheka, or the commissars in the army. He also stopped freedom of speech and in war communism he sacrificed the lives of thousands of people to get food to the troops and the workers. But this source doesn't tell me about all the good things that Lenin did. What about his land decrees and his clever decision to get Russia out of the war? I expect that's why Churchill is so critical, because he was Minister for War. You notice he says that Lenin and Trotsky were worse than the Kaiser, who was not exactly popular in Britain in 1919!

Examiner's Comments on: Answer 1

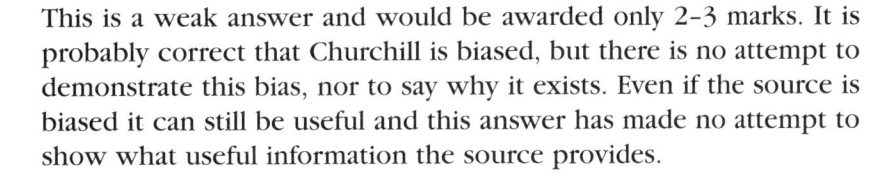

This is a weak answer and would be awarded only 2-3 marks. It is probably correct that Churchill is biased, but there is no attempt to demonstrate this bias, nor to say why it exists. Even if the source is biased it can still be useful and this answer has made no attempt to show what useful information the source provides.

Answer 2

This answer shows a good understanding of how to answer a 'How useful?' question. That is, what the source tells you, what is missing and whether you have any reason to doubt it, or believe it. This answer would score at least 8-9 marks.

16. Stalin in Power

1. Topic Summary

After Lenin's death there was a power struggle in the Soviet Union between Trotsky and Stalin to see who should lead the government. That struggle was finally won by Stalin, who then established himself in power by removing any opponents, real or imagined. Under Stalin the Soviet Union became a modern industrial nation, but only after great sacrifices by its people. There was also a great loss of personal freedom, as it was dangerous to express any complaints about the government in Stalinist Russia.

2. What do I Need to Know?

You will need to be able to answer questions on why Stalin became leader of the Communist Party instead of Trotsky and how Stalin purged the party, and later the country, of all those he saw as being against him. You will also need to know about Stalin's Five Year Plans, collectivisation, and the impact of the Second World War on the Soviet Union.

3. History of the Soviet Union, 1924–54

Stalin takes control

- After Lenin's death the country was run by the Politburo until a successor was chosen.
- Shortly before his death Lenin had described Stalin as unsuitable to replace him, but Stalin's policy of 'socialism in one country' received much more support than Trotsky's idea of world-wide revolution.
- Stalin also had the advantage of being Secretary of the Party and had friends in influential places. So it was no surprise that he gradually took control.
- By 1926 he had removed Trotsky and his supporters from the Politburo and in 1929 had him exiled from the Soviet Union. He was now in full control.

Summary box 1

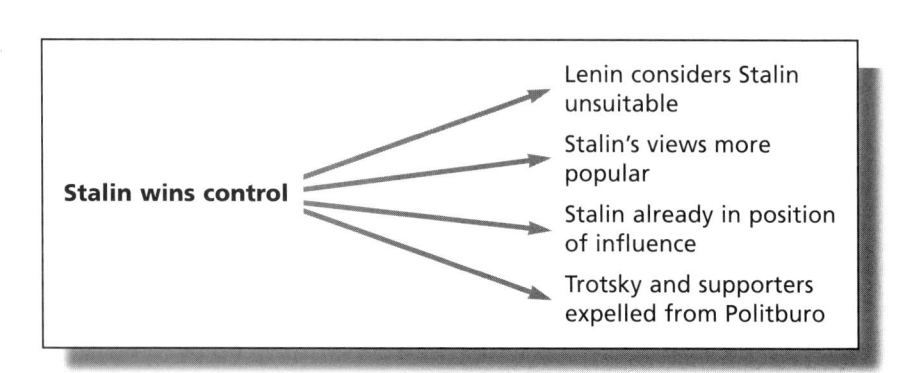

Stalin wins control
- Lenin considers Stalin unsuitable
- Stalin's views more popular
- Stalin already in position of influence
- Trotsky and supporters expelled from Politburo

Stalin and the modernisation of Russia

Success

- Stalin knew that to compete with the other major powers the Soviet Union had to bring its industries up to their level.
- He aimed to do this by using Gosplan to set a series of Five Year Plans with targets for growth in production.
- The first plan was introduced in 1928 and there were further plans beginning in 1932 and 1938. A fourth plan was introduced in 1946 to rebuild the country after the war.
- The plans were very successful and by the outbreak of the Second World War the Soviet Union was the second largest industrial power in the world. Huge steel plants had been built and railways and canals laid down to connect the new industrial areas.

Cost

- The massive increase in industrial output was achieved at the cost of personal freedom and sometimes lives.
- Many of the factory workers were peasants who had to learn new skills and disciplines. Ration cards were issued to workers and withdrawn if they went on strike or were absent from work.
- Workers were encouraged to meet unrealistically high targets and the Stakhanovites were held up as examples. When targets were not met managers could be imprisoned.
- Workers were often ordered to work on certain projects and were not able to refuse.
- Those who fell foul of the system were sent to labour camps which provided workers for schemes such as road or canal building.
- Such was the hurry to produce that goods were often of very poor quality. In the first two plans nearly 40 per cent of goods had to be rejected as faulty.
- The emphasis on industrial production meant that there was little room for producing consumer goods to improve the life of citizens. The third Five Year Plan proposed this, but had to be abandoned when war came.

Summary box 2

Plan	Cost
Need to increase production ⟶	Loss of personal freedoms
Gosplan devised Five Year Plans ⟶	Unrealistic targets
Four plans introduced ⟶	Directed labour and ration cards
Soviet Union became industrial giant ⟶	Shoddy goods
Stepped up industrial production ⟶	Little emphasis on consumer goods

Agriculture

Stalin had the most difficulty in changing the agriculture of Russia. He had two main aims for agriculture:

- To improve agricultural methods to feed the growing urban populations and industrial workers.
- To rid the Soviet Union of the Kulaks, who he thought were agricultural capitalists and an embarrassment to a communist government.

His measures to achieve these aims:

- Farms to be collectivised into Kolkhozs.
- Peasants allowed to keep small plots around their cottages.
- Government officials sent into the countryside to persuade peasants to join the new collective farms.
- Use of force against Kulaks who refused to join the collective farms. The Red Army arrested and deported millions of peasants to labour camps. Peasants who refused to join often slaughtered their animals and burned their crops in protest. So food production fell and between 1932 and 1933 there was terrible famine in which up to 10 million peasants died.

Success of collectivisation

Despite the opposition and problems collectivisation eventually worked.

- By 1937 90 per cent of Soviet farms had been collectivised.
- From 1933 agricultural production began to rise and by 1937 was significantly higher than it had been in 1928.

Summary box 3

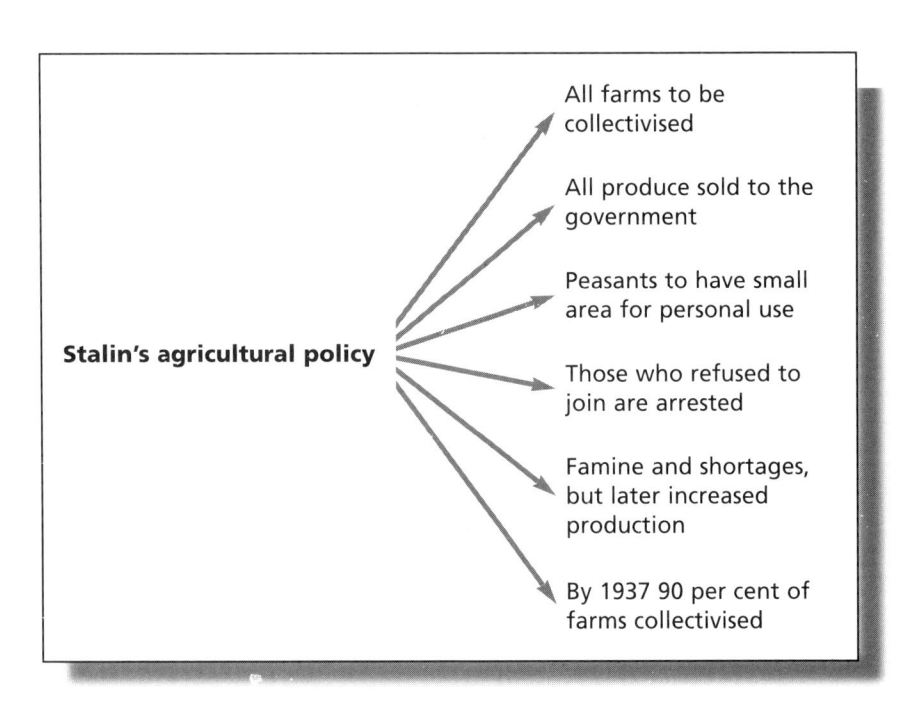

Stalin's agricultural policy
- All farms to be collectivised
- All produce sold to the government
- Peasants to have small area for personal use
- Those who refused to join are arrested
- Famine and shortages, but later increased production
- By 1937 90 per cent of farms collectivised

Dealing with the opposition

Although Stalin was completely in control in the Soviet Union by the end of the 1920s he never felt secure. His steps to deal with his opponents had tragic consequences for the Soviet people.

- Those who opposed his industrial or agricultural policies were arrested and sent to labour camps.
- Those who dared to oppose his regime in general were also sent to the camps.
- Most of Stalin's victims were 'enemies of the state', which could be anyone. An estimated 40 million were arrested between 1936 and 1953, with 24 million of them being executed in labour camps.
- Leading communists were purged, the most famous being Kamenev and Zinoviev. Many of them confessed in 'show trials' to working for Trotsky.
- By 1938 25,000 army officers had been shot, including the army's commander-in-chief.
- Millions of ordinary citizens were arrested, often after being reported by neighbours with a grudge against them.
- For some people denouncing others became a way of showing loyalty to Stalin.

Summary box 4

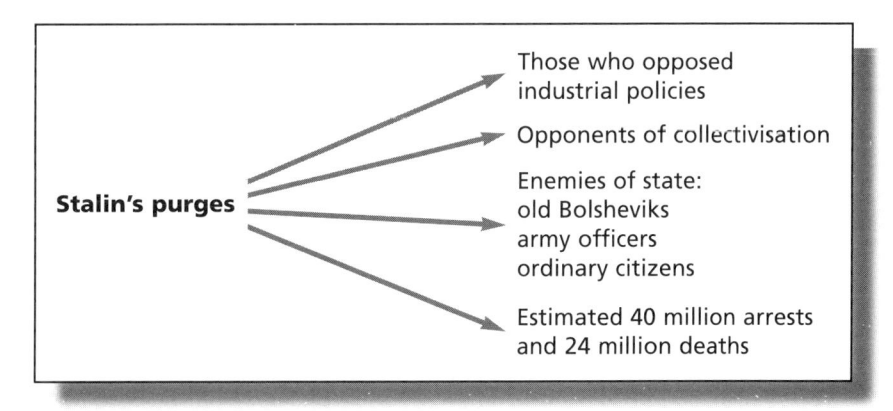

Stalin's purges:
- Those who opposed industrial policies
- Opponents of collectivisation
- Enemies of state: old Bolsheviks, army officers, ordinary citizens
- Estimated 40 million arrests and 24 million deaths

The impact of the Second World War

- In 1941 Nazi Germany invaded the Soviet Union.
- Within months the Germans were deep inside the country, but were halted in December by severe bad weather.
- In the following spring attacks began again and Leningrad resisted a German siege for 900 days, losing one million citizens.
- In January 1943 the Germans lost the battle of Stalingrad and began a slow retreat to Germany. By mid-1944 Soviet troops had cleared the country of German troops.
- Stalin emerged as a great hero for the part he played in raising morale and keeping up resistance to the Germans. For example, thousands of factories were moved east away from the areas threatened by the Germans.
- The Soviet Union survived the German invasion, but at enormous cost. Twenty million of its citizens died defending the country.

Did the Soviet Union gain from Stalin's rule?

In 1956 Stalin's successor, Khrushschev, made a speech condemning Stalin's harsh rule. But it is still possible to look at many achievements.

- His industrial and economic policies turned the Soviet Union into an industrial giant.
- His determined leadership during the Second World War helped prevented defeat by the Nazis.
- Although there was a great loss of political freedom under Stalin there were gains such as free education for all, more hospitals and doctors, new housing projects and old-age pensions.
- All this, of course, has to be balanced against the millions who died as a result of Stalin's policies or paranoia

4 What do I Know?

Once you have revised this topic thoroughly you should be able to answer most of these questions without using your notes. How many can you get right?

What was important about:
- Socialism in one country
- The Stakhanovites
- The Labour camps
- The Moscow show trials?

1. Who was Stalin's great rival for power in 1924?
2. What happened to that rival?
3. Which organisation devised the Five Year Plans?
4. When did the first Five Year Plan start?
5. Which workers were said to be a good example to other workers?
6. What was the purpose of the ration books issued to workers?
7. What percentage of industrial goods produced was faulty?
8. What was collectivisation?
9. Which group of peasants resisted it most strongly?
10. What effect did collectivisation have on industrial production?
11. How many people are thought to have been arrested in the years 1936–53?
12. Why do you think some leading politicians were arrested?
13. When did the Germans invade the Soviet Union?
14. What steps were taken to protect industrial production during the war?
15. How many Soviet citizens died in the war?

My score ....

5

Exam Type Question

Examine sources A and B. What do they tell you about life in Stalin's Soviet Union? **(10 marks)**

Source A

The judge asked 'Don't you know that Kirov was killed in Leningrad?'

I replied, 'Yes, but it wasn't I who killed him. I've never been to Leningrad.'

The judge snapped, 'Are you a lawyer or something? Kirov was killed by people who share your views, so you share the moral and criminal responsibility.'

The officials then 'withdrew for consultation' but were back within two minutes. The judge had a large sheet of paper filled with writing that must have taken twenty minutes to type. He announced the verdict. 'Ten years prison in solitary confinement.'

▲ A university lecturer giving details of her seven-minute trial for allegedly being involved in the death of Kirov.

Source B

▲ A cartoon from an American newspaper in the 1930s.

Answer 1

The sources tell us that life in Stalin's Soviet Union was really tough. Both sources are about courts and people being punished. In source A a university lecturer has been sentenced to 10 years imprisonment for a murder which she had nothing to do with. In Source B a group of well-dressed people (are they party members?) are admitting that they are guilty and the gallows are waiting at the back of the court. So obviously they are going to be executed.

Answer 2

I'm not sure how much I believe these two sources because one is by someone who spent years in prison during Stalin's reign and the other is in an American newspaper. Americans hated communism so they too had a reason to exaggerate things.

But what the sources do appear to tell us is that life in the Stalinist Soviet Union was very tough. I know that in the purges Stalin dealt with all those people who he considered to be his enemy. In source A the authorities have obviously taken the opportunity to deal with all those people who they thought were a problem. They couldn't have typed the answer up in two minutes, so obviously they had decided to find the lecturer guilty anyway. In source B we can see party members cheerfully owning up to everything. This is a reference to the show trials where old Bolsheviks pleaded guilty to crimes they probably didn't commit. They obviously knew they were going to die, but pleaded guilty to protect their families. So both sources show the sort of control that Stalin had and his desire to get rid of everyone who he thought was a threat.

Examiner's Comments on: Answer 1

This is quite a good answer. The candidate has seen that both sources involve punishments that may or may not have been deserved and that they indicate the harsh nature of law and order under Stalin. However, the candidate has failed to pick up on the significance of the quick decision in Source A or the implicit reference to the Moscow show trials in Source B. I would award this 6 marks out of 10.

Answer 2

A very good answer. The candidate uses knowledge to link the information in the sources to Stalin's purges. There is also an acknowledgement of the fact that the sources might not be entirely objective. But the candidate does not reject the sources and goes on to list what they do tell us about Soviet life. I would be happy to give this full marks.

Practice Question

Have a look at the cartoon, re-read Answer 2 and then see how well you can do it – without copying Answer 2!

The World, 1945–91

17. The Cold War

1. Topic Summary

In the period immediately after the Second World War there was a 'Cold War' between the democratic, capitalist countries of the West and the communist countries of Eastern Europe. This was not a military conflict, though it often came close to fighting. Instead it was a war of words, where propaganda was used to discredit 'the other side'. However, it also involved an arms race which brought the world to the point of nuclear destruction. The Cold War only came to an end when the Soviet Empire collapsed in 1989.

You will need to be able to explain what the Cold War was and why it came about. You will also have to explain how Europe became divided by the Iron Curtain. You will also have to explain how the conflict occurred world-wide, in places such as Vietnam and Cuba. For the most recent events exam boards will expect you to be able to explain why the once mighty Soviet Empire collapsed.

2. What do I Need to Know?

The early years, 1945–6: from ally to enemy

- During the Second World War the Soviet Union had fought on the same side as America and the other Allies. However, even before the end of the war it had become obvious that there would be disagreements between the American and Soviet 'sides'.
- The Allies had held two conferences towards the end of the war. At Yalta they had generally agreed about what was to happen at the end of the war, but at Potsdam there were serious disagreements. This was to be the beginning of a long series of disagreements called the Cold War.

3. History of the Cold War

Reasons for the Cold War

The reasons for the Cold War can be summed up in one word – distrust. Both the Soviets and the Americans simply did not trust each other. Why was this?

- They had completely different political beliefs. The Soviet Union was communist and the United States was capitalist.
- Each side was convinced that the other wanted to spread its beliefs at the expense of the other.
- During the 20th century the Soviet Union had become convinced that the West was happy to see it attacked (the examples they gave were the West sending troops to help the Whites in the Russian civil war, the reluctance of Britain to reach agreement against Hitler, and the 'unacceptable delay' in launching D-Day).

The Cold War

- The Soviet Union also thought that the dropping of the atomic bomb on Hiroshima was really a warning to them from America.
- After the Second World War each side became involved in an arms race. What was the point of building arms unless they were to be used? This increased suspicion.
- At the end of the war the Soviet Union set up a communist 'buffer zone' on its western border. The Soviets said this was a defensive measure. The Americans saw it as the first step towards world domination.

Summary box 1

Reasons for the Cold War – DISTRUST
- Capitalism vs communism
- Fear of opponents beliefs spreading
- Soviet fear that the West wanted communism crushed
- Arms race
- Establishment of communist buffer zone in Europe

Distrust in action – Europe divided

- After the war the Soviet Union made sure that communist governments were in power in Poland, Bulgaria, Albania, Yugoslavia, Czechoslovakia, Romania and Hungary. Winston Churchill said that they had made an Iron Curtain across Europe.
- The Soviets said this gave them protection against the West, but the Americans feared that as one country became communist so would the next and so on. This was the domino theory.
- So in 1947 the US President, Truman, made a speech setting out how his country would support people against communist aggression. This was called the Truman Doctrine.
- To back up their support the Americans also gave countries economic aid under the Marshall Plan. The Americans were following a policy of stopping the spread of communism. This was called containment.
- After the war Germany and its capital Berlin had been divided into four 'zones of occupation'. In 1948 the Soviets tried to take control of the whole of Berlin through the Berlin Blockade. But the other Allies were determined to stop this – and did. The Blockade lasted for nearly a year. Every day thousands of British and American planes flew in supplies to overcome the Blockade. It was a great propaganda victory when the Soviets allowed Allied lorries and trains back in.
- Shortly afterwards the area of Germany under Soviet control became East Germany and the area under Allied control became West Germany.

- Then in 1949 the West formed a military organisation under American leadership called NATO, and later the East formed an alliance called the Warsaw Pact under Soviet leadership.
- The division between East and West was further emphasised when the Soviet Union built the Berlin Wall in 1961 to stop citizens of communist East Berlin defecting to capitalist West Berlin.

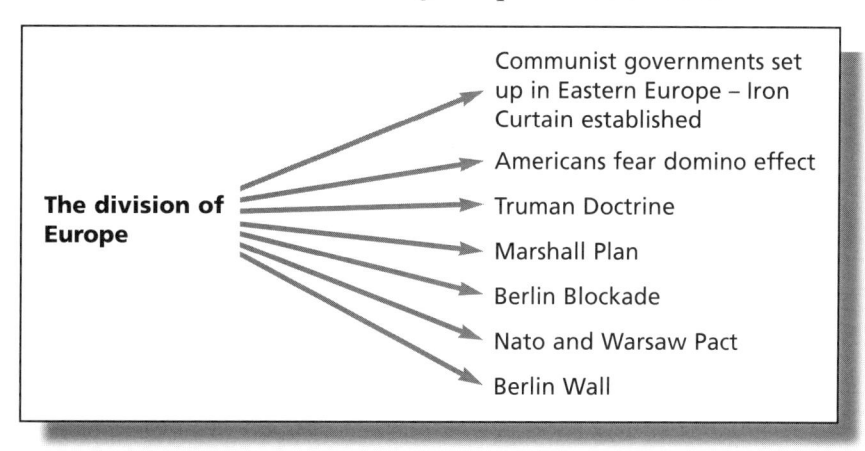

Summary box 2

The division of Europe:
- Communist governments set up in Eastern Europe – Iron Curtain established
- Americans fear domino effect
- Truman Doctrine
- Marshall Plan
- Berlin Blockade
- Nato and Warsaw Pact
- Berlin Wall

Distrust in action – around the world

The Cold War between the American-dominated West and Soviet-dominated East was not confined only to Europe.

- In 1950 communist North Korea invaded capitalist South Korea. The Americans sent troops under the banner of the United Nations to repel the North Koreans. Both communist China and the Soviet Union supported North Korea and there was a real danger of warfare between the capitalists and communists. This possibility increased when General MacArthur, commander of US forces in the Far East, threatened an attack on China. President Truman was forced to dismiss MacArthur and peace was finally agreed in 1953.
- In 1962 the Americans discovered that the Soviets had begun building nuclear missile sites on Cuba.
- The island of Cuba had once been under American control but in 1959 Fidel Castro had seized power and was carrying out reforms which looked like communism to the Americans. He had developed very good relations with the Soviet Union and was letting them station nuclear weapons on Cuba – within firing range of the USA.
- After much debate the Americans set up a naval blockade around Cuba to stop Soviet ships landing nuclear weapons on the island. If the Soviet ships sailing to Cuba had ignored that blockade, there would have been war between the two countries. Fortunately the Soviet ships turned around when the Americans made a secret promise to remove NATO missiles from Turkey (on the Soviet border).
- The USA and the Soviet Union set up a 'hotline' between Washington and Moscow to try to stop future misunderstandings, but this was a rare and short-lived thaw in the Cold War.

- After the Second World War Vietnam had become divided into communist North Vietnam and capitalist South Vietnam. Communist guerillas in South Vietnam, called the Vietcong, tried to ovethrow the government. America poured thousands of soldiers into South Vietnam to stop it becoming communist.
- The Soviet Union supported the Vietcong, as did North Vietnam. The Vietnam War dragged on until 1973, when the last American troops were pulled out after suffering enormous losses and after America lost the respect of the world. Nor did America stop the spread of communism, as North Vietnam captured South Vietnam in 1975.

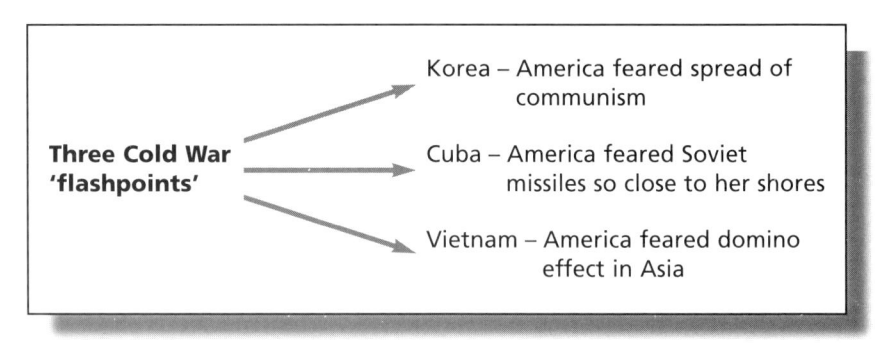

Summary box 3

Three Cold War 'flashpoints'
- Korea – America feared spread of communism
- Cuba – America feared Soviet missiles so close to her shores
- Vietnam – America feared domino effect in Asia

Distrust in Europe – Hungary and Czechoslovakia

The Soviet Union controlled Eastern Europe, but there were times when some of its communist 'allies' wanted to follow policies independent of the Soviet Union. They were not allowed to do this:

Hungary 1956

- In 1956 there were riots and strikes against the communist leader Rakosi in Hungary. He was forced to flee and the Communist Party appointed Nagy in his place.
- Nagy announced reforms and in October expelled Soviet troops from Hungary.
- The Soviet Union saw this as a threat to the Warsaw Pact and sent troops into Hungary. The Hungarians fought fiercely and awaited help from the West, but it never came.
- By mid-November the uprising was over. Thirty thousand Hungarians had died and Nagy was shot.

Czechoslovakia 1968

- In January 1968 Dubcek was elected as leader of the Communist Party in Czechoslovakia.
- He promised a number of reforms, including the freedom to travel and the end of censorship. His reforms became known as the 'Prague Spring'.
- The Soviet leader, Brezhnev, was alarmed by the reforms and in August sent Warsaw Pact troops into Czechoslovakia to remove Dubcek. Once again the West did not offer assistance to a country trying to break free from Soviet domination.

Poland 1980–1

- During the 1970s the Polish economy did well and the standard of living for many Poles was high in comparison with other communist countries.
- In the late 1970s the Polish economy collapsed and in 1980 there was a series of strikes.
- Shipworkers formed a trade union called 'Solidarity' which soon had a membership of 10 million workers. The union made a number of demands, such as the right to strike.
- Solidarity's leader, Lech Walesa, held talks with the country's prime minister, General Jarulzelski, but the Soviet Union was becoming increasingly concerned that Solidarity was becoming a political party opposed to Soviet control.
- In 1982 Jarulzelski suspended Solidarity and imprisoned Walesa.
- Later Walesa was released and in 1989 became leader of Poland – though no-one could have guessed that in 1982!

Summary box 4

The Soviet Union keeps control:
- Hungary wants reforms – crushed by Soviet tanks
- Czechs want reforms in Prague Spring – Dubcek dismissed on Soviet orders
- Poles want greater freedoms – Soviet Union pressures Polish government into arresting Solidarity leaders

The arms race

- In 1945 the Americans dropped the atomic bomb. This gave them a military supremacy over the Soviet Union which the Soviets were determined to correct.
- By 1949 the Soviet Union had the atomic bomb.
- In 1952 the Americans developed the more deadly hydrogen bomb. By 1953 the Soviets had this too.
- For the next 20 years both sides built bigger and better weapons, such as missiles with nuclear warheads which could fly from one continent to another (ICBMs). These could be launched from submarines or the back of lorries.
- By the mid-1960s each side had the capacity to destroy the other side hundreds of times over, though of course each side was frightened to use the weapons for fear of bringing about 'mutual assured destruction' (MAD!). Each side also had huge supplies of conventional weapons and hundreds of thousands of men in their armed forces.

Détente

- It seemed only logical that the sides should meet to try to limit the weapons they had – especially as both the USA and the Soviet Union were suffering from economic problems.
- In 1972 Presidents Nixon and Brezhnev began the Strategic Arms Limitation Talks (SALT) in which they agreed to reduce arms.
- In 1975 the Helsinki Agreement was made, with the countries of the East and West agreeing to inform each other when they were having military exercises.
- In 1979 the USA and the Soviet Union agreed to further reductions of arms in talks in Vienna known as SALT 2.
- Unfortunately, in the same year the Soviet Union invaded Afghanistan and the Americans boycotted the Moscow Olympics in protest. The 'détente', or relaxation of strained relations, had come to an end.
- However, in 1982 further talks began. These were Strategic Arms Reduction Talks (START) and in 1987 it was agreed to make further cuts to arms.
- However, both sides still had the ability to destroy the world at the press of a button.

Summary box 5

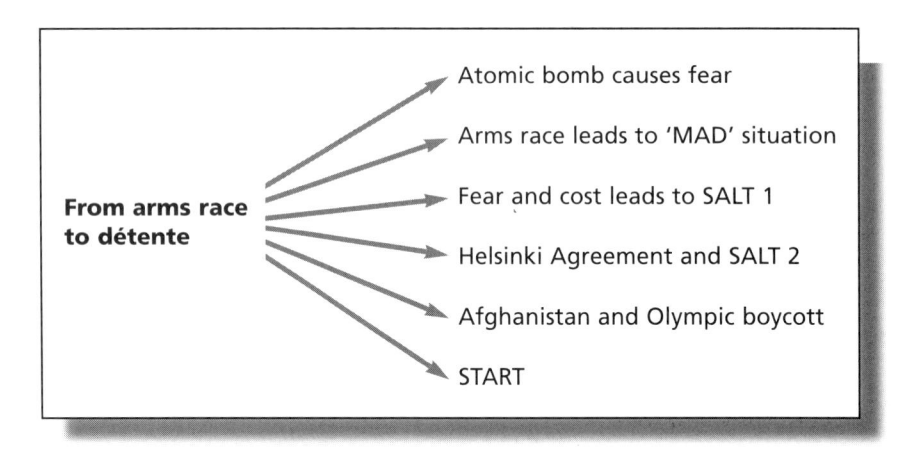

From arms race to détente
- Atomic bomb causes fear
- Arms race leads to 'MAD' situation
- Fear and cost leads to SALT 1
- Helsinki Agreement and SALT 2
- Afghanistan and Olympic boycott
- START

The Collapse of the Soviet Empire

In 1985 Michail Gorbachev became leader of the Soviet Union. He was concerned about the enormous costs of the arms race and about the poor state of the Soviet economy. He therefore put two policies into operation.

- Glasnost (openess). Gorbachev wanted to end the intense secrecy which surrounded what happened in the Soviet Union.
- Perestroika (restructuring). The time had come to open up Soviet politics to allow promotion on the grounds of efficiency (instead of party loyalty) and to allow market forces in the Soviet economy.

Part of Gorbachev's new openess involved explaining his policies to the people and trying to win their support. This new attitude also led to improved relations with the West.

- In 1989 the USA and the Soviet Union signed a treating agreeing to remove most of their missiles from Europe.
- In the same year Gorbachev informed the other Communist powers in Eastern Europe that they could no longer expect support from the Red Army.

1989, the end of communism?

By 1989 it was clear that Gorbachev's policies inside the Soviet Union were not working. The economy was in ruins and the leaders did not seem to know what to do. But in trying to relax the stranglehold of communism Gorbachev had taken the lid off a box which could not be closed again. The people of Eastern Europe saw their chance for political freedom and in a series of spontaneous uprisings overthrew their Communist rulers.

Summary box 6

Month	Country	Event
March	Hungary	The border with non-communist Austria is dismantled
June	Poland	Non-communist leader (Walesa) wins election
September	East Germany	Thousands of citizens escape to Austria and West Germany
October	East Germany	Troops refuse to fire on demonstrators
November	East Germany	Berlin Wall pulled down
November	Czechoslovakia	Demonstrations lead to opening of borders with West
December	Romania	Communist leader, Ceausescu, overthrown
December	Hungary	Free elections announced
December	Bulgaria	Mass demonstrations against communist government.

As communist governments fell across Europe it was apparent that the Cold War was over – an event perhaps symbolised by the dismantling of the Berlin Wall. Indeed, in 1991 the Warsaw Pact was formally wound up.

The Soviet Union itself lasted only a little longer. Soon republics such as Lithuania and Estonia in the Baltic and more 'mainstream' republics such as the Ukraine began demanding freedom from Soviet control. Michail Gorbachev found it increasingly difficult to maintain control, especially as in 1991 there was an attempted coup against him. Finally the Soviet Union was replaced by the Commonwealth of Independent States. Soviet Russia was now a partner not ruler of the other republics.

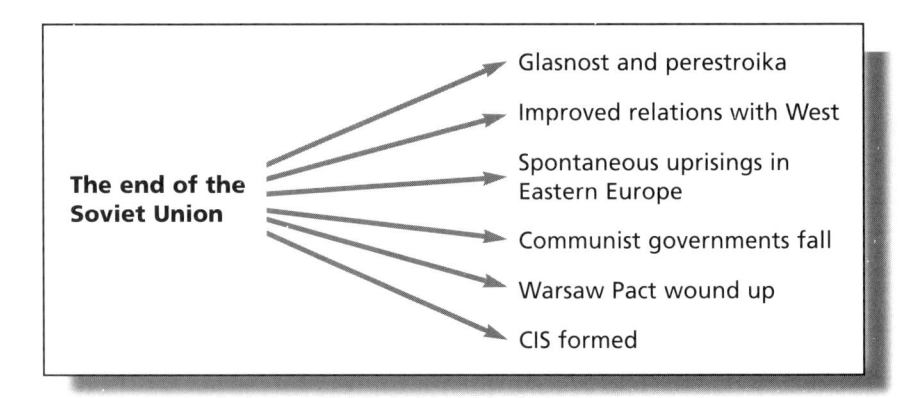

The Cold War

Summary box 7

The end of the Soviet Union:
- Glasnost and perestroika
- Improved relations with West
- Spontaneous uprisings in Eastern Europe
- Communist governments fall
- Warsaw Pact wound up
- CIS formed

4 What do I Know?

Once you have revised this topic thoroughly you should be able to answer most of these questions without using your notes. How many can you get right?

1. Which word best sums up the reasons for the Cold War?
2. Who said that an 'Iron Curtain' had descended across Europe?
3. What is the 'Domino Theory'?
4. What was the policy of containment?
5. How many zones of occupation were there in post-war Germany?
6. Which military organisation was founded by the West in 1949?
7. Who led UN forces against North Korea in the Korean War?
8. Where did the Soviet Union install nuclear weapons in 1961–2?
9. Who were the Vietcong?
10. What happened to Nagy, leader of Hungary in 1956?
11. What was the 'Prague Spring'?
12. Who led Solidarity in Poland?
13. Which Soviet leader introduced the policies of glasnost and perestroika?
14. When was the Berlin Wall pulled down?
15. Why was this event so important?

My score ………

What was important about:
- The Truman Doctrine
- The Potsdam Conference
- The Berlin Blockade
- ICBMs
- Détente
- Glasnost and perestroika?

5 Exam Type Questions

Study the two sources below and then answer these questions:
1. What is the message of Source A? **(6 marks)**
2. How similar are sources A and B? **(6 marks)**

142

The Cold War

Source A

▲ A cartoon painted on a wall in Prague in 1968.

Source B

▲ A cartoon in the *Sunday Times* in August 1980.

Question 1: Answer

The message of this cartoon is that you should not trust the army. In 1945 it was obviously being nice to the people because it has accepted the flowers from the little girl, but in 1968 it has been horrible and has shot her!

Question 2: Answer

The sources are very similar because they are both about Soviet control. In the first cartoon the Soviet soldier is shown as knocking down the little girl (representing the Czech people). The second cartoon is a little more difficult to understand. I know that the Polish people were asking for more rights in 1980 and that the Soviet Union did not approve. I expect that's why the USSR is seen trampling on the 'PO' so that it now reads 'USSRLAND'.

> Of course, there are plenty of ways in which the sources are different too. One is about Czechoslovakia and one is about Poland. The main difference though is that Source A shows that the Russians were once thought of highly and that the Czechs now feel betrayed. Source B just shows them as tough.

Examiner's Comments on: Question 1 Answer

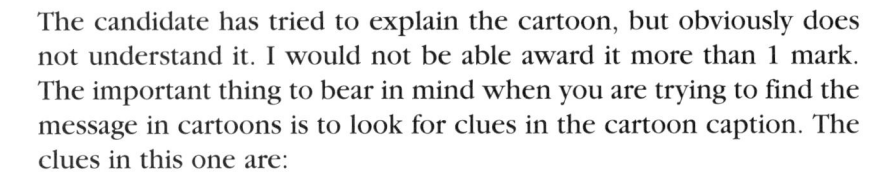

The candidate has tried to explain the cartoon, but obviously does not understand it. I would not be able award it more than 1 mark. The important thing to bear in mind when you are trying to find the message in cartoons is to look for clues in the cartoon caption. The clues in this one are:

- The cartoon is from Prague in 1968, it has two dates 1945 and 1968 and the soldier has a star on his helmet.
- Since Prague is the capital of Czechoslovakia you know the cartoon must be about that country. The star represents the Red Army. So the candidate should have been able to work out that the soldier represents the Red Army in Czechoslovakia in 1945 (when they liberated it from the Nazis) and 1968 (when they ended the 'Prague Spring').

Question 2 Answer

The candidate has the correct technique here. 'How similar' means ways in which it is similar and ways in which it is not. This is what the candidate has done. The cartoon in Source B is rather difficult and the candidate has made some intelligent comments about exactly what it means. I think this answer would score 5-6 marks.